REPEATING THE WORDS
OF THE BUDDHA

REPEATING THE WORDS OF THE BUDDHA

Tulku Urgyen Rinpoche

Foreword by Chökyi Nyima Rinpoche
Translated by Erik Pema Kunsang
Compiled & edited by Marcia Binder Schmidt

RANGJUNG YESHE ◆ BOUDHANATH, HONG KONG & ESBY ◆ 2006

Rangjung Yeshe Publications
55 Mitchell Blvd, Suite 20
San Rafael, CA 94903 USA

Address mail to:
Rangjung Yeshe Publications
C/O Above
www.rangjung.com
www.lotustreasure.com

First edition, 1992. Second edition, 2006

1 3 5 7 9 8 6 4 2

Distributed to the book trade by: Ingrams

Printed in the United States of America

Publication Data:

Tulku Urgyen Rinpoche (b. 1920–1996). Foreword by
Venerable Chökyi Nyima Rinpoche (b. 1951).

Repeating the Words of the Buddha Compiled & edited by
Marcia Binder Schmidt. Translated from the Tibetan by Erik Pema
Kunsang (Erik Hein Schmidt). 4th ed.

ISBN 13 978-962-7341-59-8 (pbk.)

1. Buddhism. 2. Vajrayana philosophy. 3. Buddhism—Tibet.
4. Oral instructions. I. Title.

Associate editor: Kerry Moran
Cover design: Michael Tweed

This book is dedicated to the Buddhadharma and all sentient beings. It is said that when the teachings of the Buddha flourish, there will be happiness for all beings in this life, in the bardo, and in following lives.

Tulku Urgyen Rinpoche

CONTENTS

Foreword by Chökyi Nyima Rinpoche 7

A MESSAGE TO PEOPLE THE WORLD OVER 13

THE FOUR DHARMAS OF GAMPOPA 17

RE-ENLIGHTENMENT 47

IMPERMANENCE 55

THE INNERMOST REFUGE 75

DEVOTION AND COMPASSION 85

VAJRASATTVA 93

THE THREE EXCELLENCES 103

OBSTACLES 115

DHARMA PRACTICE AND WORLDLY AIMS 127

BARDO 143

FOREWORD

Within Buddhism there are traditionally two approaches to studying, reflecting upon and practicing the sacred Dharma: the analytical approach of a scholar and the simple approach of a meditator.

The style of a scholar is to study numerous details and carefully reflect upon them, refining one's understanding through using the words of the Buddha, the statements of enlightened masters, and one's personal power of reasoning. By doing so one can establish a clear understanding of the real state of things as they are, the profound emptiness that is the essence of realization of all the buddhas. This is one type of approach and it is excellent.

Certain people, whose character is intellectually inclined, find it best to take this approach, especially if they harbor many thoughts and doubts, or have a tendency toward nit-picking and suspiciousness. A person with a skeptical mentality finds it very difficult to trust a genuine master, even after having met him and received the revealing pith instructions. A strong fascination with critical questioning and analyzing prevents one from following the approach of a simple meditator and from gaining an immediate certainty about the profound nature of emptiness, the basic wakefulness that is the very heart of all the buddhas. Due to these reasons some people find much greater benefit from the analytical approach of a scholar through which doubts and lack of understanding can be gradually cleared away.

Another type of person feels less inclined to study all the details of the words of the Buddha and the statements of enlightened masters, or to investigate them with the power of factual reasoning. Rather, they wish to focus directly on the very core of the awakened state—the wakefulness that perceives every possible aspect of knowledge exactly as it is—personally, within their own experience. Such people are not so interested in taking a long, winding, round-about road through detailed studies and analytical speculations; rather, they want immediate and direct realization. For such people there is the approach of pith instructions including Mahamudra and Dzogchen.

Some people express suspicion about whether these pith instructions of Mahamudra and Dzogchen are the authentic words of the Buddha, and if so, where they can be found within the canonical scriptures. Such suspicion comes from not having read the *Tripitaka* well enough, because if one studies these scriptures carefully, one finds that the intrinsic wakefulness of Mahamudra, or of Dzogchen for that matter, is described with the utmost clarity in the tantras. With only a shallow erudition in the *Tripitaka* and its commentaries (in Tibetan known as *Kangyur* and *Tengyur*), and having studied nothing more than a handful of fragments of the Buddha's words which may not explicitly contain the terms Mahamudra or Dzogchen, there is fertile ground for suspicion and doubt. In short, suspicion results from shallow learning.

The tradition of Tulku Urgyen Rinpoche and other masters of his caliber is to focus on the simple approach of a meditator, an approach that is saturated with direct, pithy instructions. This is a tradition of plainly and simply stating things as they are, while allowing the student to gain personal experience by alternating questions with advice. By being questioned repeatedly by the master, the disciple's uncertainty is gradually cleared away, so that finally the very heart of the awakened state is revealed and seen nakedly and directly.

Unless one is a completely unsuited person, when faced with such a style of instruction, one definitely does gain some feeling of certainty, an immediate assurance of how the awakened state really is. Afterwards, however, this glimpse of insight must be continued, and whether or not it is repeated and brought into personal experience depends solely upon the individual and does not lie within the master's power. The master's duty is to point out the naked state of wakefulness; to train in meditation after having recognized this naked state lies in the hands of the disciple. In this context meditation means to sustain the continuity of what was recognized, and that is totally up to us, the disciples.

Furthermore, our karmic deeds, disturbing emotions, and habitual tendencies are indeed powerful, and so we need to purify our veils and gather the accumulations of merit and wisdom. Doing such practices helps us as well to sustain the continuity.

In this way all aspects of the Buddha's teachings can be gathered into a single point. Though outwardly there are many layers, many peels—practices that help for longevity, good health, sharper intelligence, and the like—ultimately, the true benefit lies in recognizing, exactly as it is, the state of basic wakefulness that perceives all aspects of knowledge. Whether we approach spiritual practice from the angle of purifying and gathering merit, or whether we apply a meditation technique from the Vajrayana system, the different practices should, first of all, facilitate this recognition for someone who hasn't recognized. For someone who has already recognized, they should help sustain the continuity of recognition. That is the vital point of all spiritual practice.

Tulku Urgyen Rinpoche teaches in a style known as instruction through personal experience. He has spent many years in retreat, practicing in the sense of assimilating the teachings within his experience. Consequently, he speaks from experience, expressing what he himself has undergone. Such teachings are unique, and at times his way of phrasing instructions is amazing. Sometimes they are not particularly eloquent, but always his words have a strongly beneficial impact on the listener's mind. I find that just half an hour of Rinpoche's teachings is more beneficial than reading through volumes of books. That is the effect of instruction through personal experience. That is his style.

To teach that the enlightened essence is present within the mind of any sentient being; to teach how this essence is, directly, so it can be recognized within the listener's experience; to show the need for recognizing it and the tremendous benefit of doing so; to show clearly how at that moment the buddha, the awakened state, needs not to be sought for elsewhere but is present within yourself; and that you become enlightened through experiencing what was always present within you—that is what Tulku Urgyen Rinpoche teaches and that is what is written down here. I believe that there is great benefit to be gained when you read this book carefully and apply it to yourself in a very personal way.

—*Chökyi Nyima Rinpoche*

A MESSAGE TO PEOPLE THE WORLD OVER

Foremost I would like to tell you that an enlightened essence is present in everyone. It is present in every state, both samsara and nirvana, and in all sentient beings; there is no exception. Experience your buddha nature, make it your constant practice, and you will reach enlightenment. In my lifetime I have known many, many people who attained such an enlightened state, both male and female. Awakening to enlightenment is not an ancient fable. It is not mythology. It actually does happen. Bring the oral instructions into your own practical experience and enlightenment is indeed possible; it is not just a fairy tale.

To realize our buddha nature, we need the support of three principles. First is the precious Buddha, the primal teacher who showed the enlightened essence to others. Next is the precious dharma, the teachings on how to train in experiencing the enlightened essence. Lastly, there is the precious sangha, the people who uphold and spread the teachings. Additionally, there are three roots: there is the guru, the root of blessings; the yidam, the root of accomplishment; and the dakini, the root of activities. They possess all-knowing wakefulness, all-embracing compassion, the activity of deeds for the benefit of beings, and the capacity to protect and save others.

Sometimes we may have doubts and hesitation when relating to the Buddha's teachings, but do not leave it with that. It is very important to validate what is trustworthy and what is not. My teachers mentioned four kinds of validation. First are the words of a perfectly enlightened being, such as the Buddha, whose statements are never unwise. Then there are the teachings by the great masters of the lineage, passed from one to the other until today. Third are the instructions we receive from our own personal teacher. Finally, to decide with certainty, we need the validation of our own intelligence. Do not leave anything to blind faith or convential belief. Examine for yourself what is really the truth.

What is the reason for the misery and pain every living being undergoes? What is the cause of samsara's delusion? It is nothing other than lacking the experience of our enlightened essence. We ignore what is primordially present; we neglect what is continually present within us: our buddha nature. Instead, immersed in confused emotions, we chase illusory aims that endlessly result in more deluded experience. That's called samsara. We have already done that for countless lifetimes, life after life, death following rebirth. Unless you now take this opportunity, while you are still a human being, to realize what is fully possible, you will continue in the future in the same deluded way.

Please understand that the buddha nature is present within everyone. Nobody lacks this potential, not even a single person in this world. Unless you learn how to bring it into your personal experience, train in that and realize it, you remain deluded. Delusion never disappears by itself. Spinning around on the rim of samsara's vicious wheel, on the twelve links of dependent origination, you will continue life after life. We all die, are reborn, and die again, countless times.

But, in this present life, you can learn to experience your enlightened essence, and if you do that, you can, before passing away, attain the perfectly and fully awakened state of a buddha. The method to transform this human body into rainbow light at the moment of death is only through recognizing and realizing our buddha nature; there is no other possible way. The instruction for how to do that is still available. Place your trust in the three jewels: the precious Buddha, dharma and sangha. Receive this teaching from someone who holds an unbroken lineage; this lineage is still intact. Otherwise, everyone dies; there is no exception. In the past, everyone who lived in this world died. Right now everyone alive will die. Everyone born in the future will also die. Everything in the world changes; nothing remains the same, nothing is permanent, nothing lasts. If you want to be successful, if you really want to take care of yourself— recognize your enlightened essence.

THE FOUR DHARMAS
OF GAMPOPA

Grant your blessings that my mind may follow the Dharma.
Grant your blessings that my Dharma practice may become the
path.
Grant your blessings that the path may clarify confusion.
Grant your blessings that confusion may dawn as wisdom.

Gampopa

Since I do not possess any qualities of learning or accomplishment, I will simply repeat the flawless words of the Buddha in order to benefit those who show sincere interest in the Dharma.

The incomparable and world-renowned great master Gampopa condensed all the teachings that have been given and will be given by the one thousand buddhas in this good eon into four sentences known as the Four Dharmas of Gampopa. These extremely profound sentences are a combination of Sutra and Tantra, and were expounded upon by the great master Longchen Rabjam. If a practitioner receives these instructions and is diligent, he or she will be able to attain complete enlightenment within a single lifetime. It is amazing how extraordinary the vital teachings of the buddhas and accomplished practitioners are.

The buddhas have totally perfected all the qualities of abandonment and realization; they have abandoned the veils and realized the wisdom qualities. Out of their great love and kindness for other beings, similar to the love a mother has for her only child, the awakened ones taught the Dharma. The source of Buddhism on this earth is Buddha Shakyamuni, the completely enlightened one. His teachings have been transmitted through a lineage of bodhisattvas abiding on the bhumis, the bodhisattva levels. Thus these teachings have been passed down through an unbroken lineage of accomplished practitioners up to my own root teacher.

The first of the Four Dharmas of Gampopa is "Grant your blessings that my mind may follow the Dharma!" This is done by reflecting on the four mind-changings. The first of these describes the difficulty of obtaining a precious human body endowed with the eight freedoms and ten riches. Since we are already human beings it might seem that we effortlessly obtained a human body; however, that was not the case. It takes a tremendous amount of positive karma accumulated in former lifetimes for an individual to be born in a precious human body. There are as many human beings as there are stars in the sky at night. But among these humans, those who have interest in practicing the sacred Dharma, beings with a precious human body, are extremely few, like the stars in the morning sky. Among people with interest in Dharma, those who have sincere diligence are even less. Genuine Dharma practice means to give up all worldly ambitions and to pursue instead the attainment of complete enlightenment in this very lifetime.

Although we have obtained a precious human body, it is governed by impermanence. Impermanence means that nothing, neither the world nor the beings in it lasts. In particular, the life span of a human is extremely short, as unpredictable and insubstantial as a flash of lightning or a bubble in water. On this earth no one lives forever; one after the other, people pass away. After death, if we end up in the three lower realms we will undergo unbearable, indescribable misery and pain. Currently we strive for perfect conditions, pleasure and wealth. But no matter what incredible state of worldly luxury and happiness we might now attain, we lack the power to bring any of it—our friends, family members or wealth—into the afterlife.

Although we feel love and affection for our family and our friends, at the moment of death we journey alone to an unknown place. We have repeated the same experience in all our past lives, leaving behind all our acquaintances and abandoning our possessions. No matter what happiness and abundance we achieve in this lifetime, it is as insubstantial as the dream we dreamt last night. To understand that nothing lasts, that everything passes by like a dream, is to understand impermanence and death.

If it simply were the case that our life ended in nothingness, like water drying up or a flame being extinguished, that would be perfect. There wouldn't be anything to worry about. But I'm sorry to say it does not happen like that, because our consciousness is not something that can die. After death we are forced to experience the effect of our former karmic actions. Due to ignorance we have wandered endlessly in samsara, unable to be liberated, continually circling between the three lower and three higher realms, one after the other. In order to free ourselves from the six realms of samsaric existence, we need to practice the sacred Dharma now while we have the chance.

We continue in samsaric existence as long as we are covered by the emotional obscurations and the cognitive obscurations. These two obscurations are precisely what hinder us from attaining the state of omniscient buddhahood. In order to remove them we engage in the practices known as the preliminaries. These practices are included under Gampopa's second teaching, "Grant your blessings that my Dharma practice may become the path." First we take refuge and do prostrations, thereby removing the karmic misdeeds and obscurations of our body gathered in countless lifetimes. In order to remove the negative actions and obscurations of speech which we have accumulated since beginningless time, we practice the meditation and recitation of Vajrasattva. To remove the obscurations and negative actions of our mind gathered during beginningless lifetimes, we make the outer, inner and secret mandala offerings. Finally, to remove the negative actions and obscurations which have been gathered through a combination of body, speech and mind from beginningless time, we practice the outer, inner and secret aspects of guru yoga. It is said that "realization occurs spontaneously when the obscurations are removed." Guru yoga is an extremely profound practice which is excellent for removing obscurations and developing realization. Though it is placed among the preliminary practices, it is said to be more profound than the main part of practice itself.

Gampopa's teaching is "Grant your blessings that the path may clarify confusion." Here, "path" should be understood within the context of ground, path, and fruition, a structure that encompasses all the teachings of Sutra and Tantra. The ground is the buddha nature, *sugata-garbha*, the dharmakaya of all the buddhas that is present in all sentient beings. It is compared to pure, undefiled gold endowed with supreme qualities and free from any defects. How is the buddha nature present in everyone? The example given is that of oil in a mustard seed. When pressed, a mustard seed always yields oil. In the same way, in all sentient beings there is the essence of buddhahood, the buddha nature. No one lacks it. All the buddhas and bodhisattvas have buddha nature, as well as all sentient beings down to the tiniest insect, without any difference whatsoever in size or quality.

The buddha nature encompasses all of samsara and nirvana. Space is beyond center and edge. Wherever space pervades there are sentient beings. Wherever there are sentient beings buddha nature is present. That is what is meant by the statement that buddha nature encompasses all of samsara and nirvana, all worlds, all beings.

Although buddha nature is present in everyone, we fail to recognize it. This ignorance is the main cause for wandering in samsara. Due to the ignorance of not knowing their own nature, sentient beings have strayed into confusion, like pure gold that has fallen into the mud and is temporarily defiled. Buddhas did not stray into confusion but retained their 'natural seat'. The difference between buddhas and sentient beings is the difference between knowing or not knowing our innate nature.

Although gold is gold, when it falls in the mud it gets covered by dirt and becomes unrecognizable. Gold temporarily covered by mud is the example for sentient beings who fail to recognize their own nature. All sentient beings are buddhas, but due to temporary obscurations they do not realize it. The ground is likened to pure gold, while the path is like gold which has fallen in the dirt and is covered by defilements. In this context, the path means the state of confusion.

Buddhahood, the realized state of all awakened beings, means not straying onto the path of confusion but recognizing the state of the ground as being pure gold. Due to the power of confusion we have now strayed onto the state of the path—the pure gold is temporarily covered by mud. We are temporarily under the power of confusion. Because of the sleep of ignorance, we go through the dreams of the three realms, taking rebirth among the six classes of sentient beings again and again, endlessly.

Intrinsic to our buddha nature are qualities known as the three kayas or the innate body, speech and mind, also known as the three vajras. The vajra body is the unchanging quality of the buddha nature; the vajra speech is its inexpressible, unceasing quality; and the vajra mind is its unmistaken quality. In this way the vajra body, vajra speech, and vajra mind are inherently present as our buddha nature.

At this time the unchanging vajra body is obscured by our transient, perishable, physical body. The unceasing, continuous vajra speech, the voice of the nature of equality, is temporarily obscured by the repeated utterances of our normal talk. Likewise, the unmistaken vajra mind is obscured by our deluded thinking. Although the body, speech and mind of all the victorious ones are present in our buddha nature, they are obscured by our ordinary body, speech and mind.

Since we are under the power of confusion we are at the state of the path. Teachings are given in order to let the path clarify this confusion, thus purifying the obscurations of our body, speech and mind. The different practices taught are: development stage, to visualize our body as the form of the buddhas; recitation stage, to chant the mantras with our voice; and completion stage, to let our mind rest in the state of samadhi.

Development stage or visualization does not mean to imagine something which is not already present. The vajra body of all the victorious ones is within ourselves, intrinsic to our buddha nature. By practicing the development stage we remove the veil that covers this nature and prevents us from realizing it. The unceasing vajra speech of all the buddhas, the king of all melodious expressions, is also present in ourselves. Recitation of the three types of mantra—*vidya, dharani,* and *guhya*—enables us to remove the obscuration of our ordinary voice. The mind of all the buddhas, nonconceptual wakefulness, is also inherent to our nature, but it is covered by our momentary conceptual thinking. Simply resting in the evenness of the state of samadhi reveals our innate vajra mind.

Do not consider development stage to involve imagining something which is not real, like pretending that a piece of wood is pure gold. Development stage is not at all like that. It is simply acknowledging what already is, what already exists. Development stage means to mentally create or imagine the form of the buddhas. Even though visualization is at this point an artificial construct, a mentally fabricated act, still it is an imitation that resembles what is already present in ourselves. Until we are able to practice the ultimate development stage, we need to visualize or mentally create pure images in order to approach that absolute state.

The ultimate development stage involves simply resting in the essence of mind of all the buddhas, out of which the two form kayas—the sambhogakaya of rainbow light and the nirmanakaya of a physical body—spontaneously manifest. In fact, the buddha nature is the starting point for development stage, and this innate nature is actualized through practicing the samadhi of suchness. Development stage is created out of the samadhi of suchness, which is the dharmakaya of all the buddhas. Out of dharmakaya unfolds sambhogakaya, which is the samadhi of illumination, and from sambhogakaya the nirmanakaya appears by means of the samadhi of the seed syllable. That is how the development stage should take place.

The samadhi of suchness is the recognition of the buddha nature itself, the flawless and primordially pure state of dharmakaya. If we have not recognized this nature in our personal experience, we can approximate or fabricate it by imagining that all phenomena, all worlds and beings, dissolve into emptiness, by chanting, for instance, the mantra OM MAHA SHUNYATA JNANA VAJRA SVABHAVA ATMA KOH HANG. Out of the great emptiness, the clarity of cognizance unfolds like the sun rising in the sky and spreading light. That is the samadhi of illumination, which is in essence the sambhogakaya. Out of space there is sunlight, and from the sunlight a rainbow appears. This is the analogy for nirmanakaya, the samadhi of the seed syllable from which the form of the deity manifests. Nirmanakaya is visible but not tangible; we cannot take hold of it with our hands and yet it appears. We should imagine the form of the deity as apparent but without self-nature. Just as a rainbow in the sky is not substantial or material in any way whatsoever, the deity is not composed of flesh and blood.

To reiterate, the development stage takes place within the framework of the three kayas. Dharmakaya is all-pervasive like space. Within the space of dharmakaya, the sambhogakaya is vividly present like the light of the sun. Nirmanakaya appears like a rainbow to accomplish the welfare of beings. Just as the sun cannot rise and shine without the openness of space, the unceasing sambhogakaya cannot manifest without the nonarising nature of dharmakaya. Without space the sun cannot shine; without sunshine a rainbow cannot appear. In this way the three kayas are indivisible.

Thus, the practice of the three samadhis provides the framework for visualizing the deity. Next, we invoke the ultimate deity from the realm of Akanishtha and dissolve it inseparably into ourselves. Then we make praises and offerings and so forth. All these seemingly conventional activities in the development stage resemble the activities of ordinary human beings, just like when we invite important people to visit, praise them, and give them good food and presents. The purpose of the development stage is to purify our habitual tendencies as human beings. It is not to appease some external gods by giving them offerings. Deities are not subject to pleasure when being worshipped or displeasure when not; it is we who benefit by purifying our obscurations and gathering the accumulations.

When practicing development stage, do it with a sense of vastness, immensity and openness. Don't visualize the deity in your own little house, in this little world. Everything is first dissolved totally into great emptiness, into vast space. Within the vastness of space, the mandala of the five elements is created. On top of it we imagine the immense Mount Sumeru. At the summit of Mount Sumeru is the celestial palace, and inside it is the throne with a seat of a sun and moon disk. It is on top of this throne that we appear in the form of the yidam deity, whichever it may be. This is how we should practice the development stage, not imagining we are sitting in our own little room.

The main purpose of development stage is to destroy our clinging to a solid reality. It is our fixation on concreteness that makes us continue in samsaric existence. The development stage dismantles that. How do we approach that? By imagining the world is a buddhafield, our dwelling place is the celestial palace, and the beings in it are the divine forms of deities, visible yet intangible like a rainbow in the sky.

Similarly, the recitation of mantra destroys our fixation on our normal discontinuous speech, which stops and starts. Mantra is known as the king of verbal expression. It is the unceasing vajra speech. Finally, the unmistaken vajra mind destroys our normal conceptual thinking.

At the end of the period of recitation comes the completion stage, which in this context is the dissolution of the palace and the deity into emptiness and the re-emerging from the state of emptiness in the form of the deity. The purpose of dissolving is to eliminate our habitual fixation on appearances as being real and permanent, as well as the tendency towards the view of eternalism. By re-emerging in the visible yet insubstantial form of the deity we also destroy the basis for nihilism, the view that nothing whatsoever exists. Thus, by training in eliminating the tendencies for both wrong views, this practice truly is the path that clarifies confusion.

In short, this was about how to let the path clarify confusion. At present we are under the power of confusion. Through these practices we will be able to eradicate this confusion and realize the vajra body, speech, and mind of all the buddhas. A good metaphor for this confusion is the hallucinations caused by the psychedelic drug datura. Normally we see ourselves and other people as having one face, two arms and two legs. But when intoxicated by datura, all of a sudden we see people not as they are but with ten heads, twenty arms, fifty legs, or the like. Currently we are under the influence of the drug of ignorance and continue deluded within the six realms of samsara. When the effect of datura wears off, we again perceive people as they are in their natural state. But right now the effect of the drug of ignorance has not yet worn off; we are still under the power of confusion. In order to clarify confusion on the path we need to practice the stages of development, recitation, and completion.

Gampopa's fourth teaching, "Grant your blessings that confusion may dawn as wisdom" refers to the completion stage. The earlier mention of the completion stage is defined by and dependent upon a visualization that is either dissolved into emptiness or re-appears from emptiness; thus it is called completion stage with attributes. The true completion stage, the topic of Gampopa's fourth teaching, involves recognizing our buddha nature. When pure gold is covered by dirt it is not obvious that it is gold, even though this dirt is temporary. But once it is removed we realize that the gold is gold. In the same way, when our confusion is purified, the wisdom which is our basic wakefulness is made manifest.

At present the state of ordinary people is like pure gold covered with dirt. Our buddha nature is covered by temporary obscurations. One of the main veils that needs to be purified is our fixation on duality, on solid reality. Once it is purified then gold is just pure gold. As long as our mind is confused, bewildered, deluded, and mistaken, our buddha nature continues to be dragged through the realms of samsara. But when the mind is unconfused, unmistaken, and undeluded, it is the buddha nature itself. It is not that the buddha nature is one thing and our mind is another separate thing. They are not two different entities. The undeluded mind itself is the pure gold, the buddha nature. Sentient beings do not have two minds. When the mind is deluded it is given the name 'sentient being.' When the mind is undeluded, unmistaken, it is known as buddha.

It is said that "there is no buddha apart from your own mind." We do not have two minds. There is just one mind which is either deluded or undeluded. The buddha nature is exactly the originally unmistaken quality of our mind, also known as Samantabhadra, the dharmakaya buddha.

According to one system, the dharmakaya aspect of this primordially unmistaken quality is Samantabhadra. Its sambhogakaya aspect is Vajradhara and its nirmanakaya aspect is Vajrasattva. For example, space, sunlight, and the appearance of a rainbow are impossible to separate. Sunshine does not manifest anywhere else than within space, and a rainbow does not occur in any way other than as a combination of space and sunlight. Dharmakaya is likened to space, sambhogakaya to sun, and nirmanakaya to the rainbow. In the same way, the three buddhas, Samantabhadra, Vajradhara, and Vajrasattva, are not three different enlightened beings. They are indivisible, of the same nature, just as the three kayas are inherently present, indivisibly, in our buddha nature.

There is a difference between being deluded and undeluded, between recognizing and not recognizing our nature. The primordially unmistaken quality is known as enlightenment, buddhahood, or the awakened state of dharmakaya. The primordially deluded aspect is called ignorance, or the deluded experience of sentient beings. Although we have the essence of buddhahood within us, it is temporarily obscured.

The essence of the Buddha's teachings is the method on how to let confusion dawn as wisdom. The most vital point here is the introduction to and recognition of the buddha nature, the innate wisdom of dharmakaya that is already present within oneself. The Fourth Dharma of Gampopa is a teaching on how to recognize, train in, and stabilize this recognition of the buddha nature. Understanding it is known as the view, practicing it is called samadhi, and stabilizing it is buddhahood. Buddhahood is not outside. It is not something else that all of a sudden is absorbed into ourselves and magically transforms us into a buddha.

We have one mind but we need to distinguish between its two aspects: essence and expression. Understand this example for the relationship between the two. The essence is like the sun shining in the sky. The expression is like its reflection upon the surface of water. The sun in the sky is the real sun. The reflection of the sun appearing on the surface of water looks like the sun but is not the real sun. Let's call the sun in the sky the buddha nature, the unmistaken, undeluded quality, the essence itself. The reflection of the sun upon the surface of water is an example for our normal deluded thinking, the expression. Without the sun in the sky it is impossible for a reflection of the sun to appear. Although there is actually only one sun, it looks like there are two. It is one identity with two aspects. The essence, the buddha nature, is like the sun shining in the sky. The expression is our thinking, which is compared to the sun's reflection.

The state of being a buddha is unconfused and un-deluded, just like the sun shining in the sky. The state of mind of sentient beings is like the reflection of the sun on water. Just as the reflection is dependent upon water, our thoughts are dependent upon objects. The object is what is thought of, the subject is the perceiving mind. Subject-object fixation is the cause for continuing in deluded samsaric existence, day and night, life after life. The fixation upon subject and object, the perceiving subject and the perceived object, is solidified again and again each moment and thus re-creates samsaric existence. Right now we have the five sense objects of sights, sounds, smells, tastes, and textures. In between, as the gates, we have the five senses, and there are also the various con-sciousnesses which continuously apprehend these differ-ent sense objects.

Can the reflection of the sun on the water illumi-nate the whole world? Can it even shine over the whole lake? Can it make things grow? No, because it does not have the qualities of the real sun. In the same way, the aspect of mind known as expression, our thinking, lacks the qualities of the real state of buddhahood. But the sun in the sky by itself is able to shine and spread its warmth throughout the whole world, illuminating all darkness. To put it simply, the mind of the buddhas is unobscured, while the mind of sentient beings is obscured. What is the obscuration? It is our own reoccurring fixation on subject and object.

Buddha nature is continuously present in ourselves as well as in everyone else, without any exception whatsoever. It is in essence forever unobscured. It doesn't increase or decrease. It is not sometimes covered or uncovered. It is totally beyond mental constructs. It does not change in size. It is not that someone has a big buddha nature and somebody else a small one. There is no difference in quality either. It is continuously present to the same extent in everyone.

To recognize the buddha nature present in oneself is known as the view. To sustain the continuity of that correctly is called meditation or training. To mingle that with daily activities and act in accordance with the Dharma is action or conduct. And to realize it as totally unobscured, like the sun shining with unchanging brilliance in the sky, is known as fruition. We need to recognize the view; we need to recognize our buddha nature. Although it is something we already have, we need to acknowledge what we possess. The preliminary practices, the development stage, and so forth are all meant to enable us to recognize the buddha nature. They are like helpers, assistants.

To say "recognize your own nature, the buddha nature!" does not mean that we have to produce something which does not exist, like trying to squeeze gold out of a piece of wood, which is impossible. We must simply recognize what we already possess. But humans, who are the most clever and capable of all the different types of sentient beings, seem to be bent on totally throwing away this most precious wish-fulfilling jewel. The normal state of a human being is like someone who has found a precious wish-fulfilling jewel but ignores it, thinking that a fake piece of jewelry is more valuable. There is nothing sadder or of greater waste than this.

Think very well about this. Try to understand that the situation we are in now is like holding a wish-fulfilling jewel right in our hand. It is not easy to take rebirth as a human being, and it is definitely not easy to gain a precious human body with its opportunity to practice the Dharma. It is an extremely rare occasion that occurs so infrequently that it's like enjoying a good meal once in a hundred years. If we had a good meal only once every century, wouldn't we truly appreciate it and be overjoyed, saying "Finally I got a delicious meal!" We would be so happy. But this opportunity is even more precious. No amount of good meals is going to help us, ultimately. The body is still a corpse when it dies, whether or not it ate well. The precious human body is something extremely rare. If we do not use the opportunity we have right now, there is no guarantee whatsoever that we will be human in our next life. In fact, it is almost certain that we will not, because the habitual negative karmic patterns are so strong. This short opening right now will soon be covered up again for eons and eons before we have another chance to be a human. Please think sincerely about this: is there any greater waste than throwing away a wish-fulfilling jewel when you finally find one?

If we didn't already have this wish-fulfilling jewel it would be difficult to find. But, as a matter of fact, through all our beginningless lifetimes we have never been without it. If we were told, "You must possess a wish-fulfilling jewel!", then we would be in trouble because we would suddenly have to come up with something we don't possess. But the wish-fulfilling jewel of buddha nature is already present in ourselves. It is because of our ignorance and delusion that we do not recognize it, and continue life after life among the six classes of sentient beings. How sad that people throw away what is really valuable and instead chase after food, wealth, good reputation, and praise. But if we do not take hold of what is truly valuable in this lifetime we will just continue endlessly in samsaric existence. I'm not asking you to understand this, because of course you already do; I'm simply reminding you.

The buddha nature is already present as the nature of our own mind, just like the unchanging brilliance of the sun shining in the sky. But due to our ordinary dualistic thinking, this sun of the buddha nature is not evident; we don't see it. Not even a fraction of the innate qualities of buddhahood are manifest in the state of mind of a normal person. The conceptual thoughts we have day and night obscure our buddha nature, just like the sun in the sky is momentarily covered by clouds and seems to be obscured. Due to the passing clouds of ignorance we do not recognize the buddha nature.

The ever-present buddha nature is like the unhindered sun shining in the sky, but sunshine never reaches inside a cave facing north. This cave is an example for misunderstanding, wrong view, or partial understanding.

Buddha nature is primordially all-pervasive, present in everyone from Buddha Samantabhadra down to the tiniest insect. This enlightened essence can be given different names: dharmakaya, Samantabhadra, self-existing wakefulness or supreme enlightenment. The ignorant state of sentient beings has also many names—it is called thinking, conceptual mind, dualistic consciousness or intellect.

Before this life we were born in another place and before that life somewhere else, and so on. We have had countless previous lifetimes. Our mind did not spontaneously appear out of nothing. It is beginningless. Our mind has taken birth again and again since beginningless time. We have had countless lifetimes—and now we have reached this life. It is like a dividing point in the road where we can take a path that leads either up or down.

Our mind creates virtue and evil, and our voice and body act as the mind's servants or employees. What is meant here by evil? It is basically attachment, anger and dullness. I have explained enlightened mind; now I will point out dualistic mind.

Take for example visual objects. When we see a beautiful piece of brocade, at first glance we think "How nice!" That is attachment. If we see a used handkerchief we don't like it. That is aversion or anger. If we see a clean plain handkerchief we don't care much either way. That is indifference or dullness. We are all alike in this respect: when we see something beautiful, we like it, something ugly we dislike it, and something neutral we don't care about it. We like melodious sounds, not harsh, unpleasant ones. Our liking is attachment, our dislike is aversion, anger, and our indifference is dullness. Our reactions are the same with regard to what we eat, smell, or touch. Those three basic negative emotions manifest in relation to our five senses and the outer sense objects. The subject, our mind within, likes pleasure, dislikes pain, and can also remain indifferent. These six types of experience—visual form, sound, smell, taste, texture and mental objects—are known as the six collections of consciousness.

From primordial time until this very moment, the main actions we have performed have been the activities of the three poisons—attachment, anger, and dullness. We have continuously engaged in liking, disliking and remaining indifferent, not just in one or two lives, but throughout countless lifetimes. This was the instruction pointing out dualistic mind.

"Mind beyond concepts" refers to the situation of being free of the three poisons. A normal person is totally engrossed in the three poisons through his whole lifetime. To attain liberation from samsara we need to leave behind the three poisons. How can we be free from them? We cannot bury them underground, flush them away, burn them, blow them up or even throw a nuclear bomb at them and expect the three poisons to disappear. Our continuous involvement with them is like an evil machine. The perfect Buddha described samsaric existence as an ocean of endless suffering, or like the continuous revolving of an evil machine, like a vicious circle. Buddha told us we need to apply a method in order to liberate ourselves and all other sentient beings from the ocean of samsara.

The primary cause of samsaric existence is our own dualistic mind, as I just pointed out. Some people might claim, "I don't commit any evil! I don't kill, I don't steal and I don't lie. I don't do any negative actions!" While we might not perform such coarse negative actions, subtle negative actions are continuously created in our mind. As long as our liking, disliking and indifference are not purified, they block the path to liberation and complete enlightenment. So what can clear away and eradicate the three poisons in our own mind? The recognition of buddha nature, self-existing awareness.

This self-existing awareness is itself the path followed by all the buddhas of the three times. The buddhas of the past followed the path of self-existing wisdom, *rangjung yeshe*, and attained enlightenment. The buddhas of the present follow the path of self-existing wisdom, and in the future anyone who attains enlightenment will do so only by recognizing self-existing wisdom. There is not even an atom of any other path that leads to true enlightenment.

Let's take another example: imagine a room that had been completely sealed off and has remained in complete darkness for ten thousand years. The ignorant state of mind of a normal person who does not recognize the nature of mind, the buddha nature, is like the dense darkness inside that room. The moment of recognizing self-aware wisdom is like pressing the switch to turn on the light in the room that has been dark for ten thousand years. In that instant all the darkness is gone, right? Ten thousand years of darkness are dispelled in one moment. In the same way, the wisdom of recognizing one's nature dispels eons of ignorance and negative actions. When you press the switch to turn on the light in a room that has been dark for ten thousand years, doesn't the darkness disappear at once? Understand that example.

If all the windows and the doors in the room were closed we would be unable to see anything, but when the light comes on we can see everything perfectly clearly. It is possible to purify countless eons of negative karma and attain the state of complete enlightenment in this very lifetime because self-existing wisdom is so potent, so effective.

Now I will give a name to our buddha nature. It is called empty and cognizant self-existing wakefulness. The empty aspect, the essence, is like space that pervades everywhere. But inseparable from this empty quality is a natural capacity to cognize and perceive, which is basic wakefulness. Buddha nature is called self-existing because it is not made out of anything or created by anyone. Self-existing means uncreated by causes in the beginning and undestroyed by circumstances in the end. This self-existing wakefulness is present in all beings without a single exception. Our thinking and self-existing wakefulness are never apart. The thinking mind is called expression, while the basic wakefulness is known as essence. Thus there are actually two names for the mind. In the case of an ignorant sentient being the mind is called empty cognizance with a core of ignorance. The mind of all the buddhas is empty cognizance with a core of awareness.

In order to enable us to recognize or know our own essence, the teacher, the vajra master, gives the pointing-out instruction. It is for that single purpose. And yet, what he points out is not something we don't already have. We already possess the buddha nature.

First, we must recognize our own nature, our essence. Next we must endeavor with great diligence to continuously sustain that recognition, which is known as training. Finally, to reach the state where not even an iota of conceptual thinking remains, when conceptual thinking is totally purified, is called the attainment of stability. This stability is also known as the complete enlightenment of buddhahood.

The teachings of both Mahamudra and Dzogchen give a traditional example for this sequence. On the first day of the lunar calendar when we look in the sky we don't see anything; the moon is invisible. But on the evening of the third day we see a sliver of the moon. At that time it is possible for someone to point at the moon and say, "There is the moon!" We look and we see that the moon is the moon. That is called recognizing. Each following day the moon grows larger and larger, until on the night of the fifteenth day it is totally full and brilliant, shining in the sky. That is the example for the dharmakaya of self-existing awareness free from constructs. Again, pointing out the moon is known as recognizing. That it grows further and further is training. When it is finally a full, complete moon, that is the attainment of stability, complete enlightenment.

Another example is the seed of a flower. Knowing it's a seed is the example for recognizing our buddha nature. After it has been planted and watered and starts to sprout leaves, stamen, and petals, that is called training. When the flower is finally fully grown, with beautiful, multicolored blossoms, that is the example for the attainment of stability. The seed of a flower does not look like a flower in full bloom. But a seed which is unmistakenly the seed of a beautiful flower can be planted and it will grow into one.

Although when we see a flower it is amazingly beautiful, we wouldn't find the seed of that flower spectacular at all. In the same way, do not expect the recognition of mind essence to be something spectacular. But when the recognition has been stabilized, as in the case of a buddha, the state of complete enlightenment contains many great qualities like the fourfold fearlessnesses, the ten powers, the eighteen unique qualities, and so forth. The state of buddhahood also contains the capacity to transform an instant into an eon and an eon into an instant. The qualities of buddhahood are inconceivable, and all these qualities are inherently present in the buddha nature. They are not some new qualities that are achieved later on. There are not two different types of buddha nature—it is not that the buddhas have one type of buddha nature and we sentient beings have another type.

Humans are as numerous as stars at nighttime, but those with precious human bodies are like stars in the morning. All of you are like morning stars. Although I needn't ask you to treasure this teaching, to regard it as really important, still it is necessary to repeat that the practice of recognizing buddha nature should continue throughout our lives. We must equalize life and practice. In other words, we should not only practice for a short time and then abandon the Dharma. We should train for as long as we live.

RE-ENLIGHTENMENT

The confusion that arose on the state of the path can be cleared away. When we remove the temporary stains from primordially awakened rigpa, we become re-enlightened instead of primordially enlightened. This is accomplished by following the oral instructions of a qualified master.

Tulku Urgyen Rinpoche

Unfortunately all sentient beings are not one; they don't become enlightened when one person does. Individual karmas and habitual patterns are innumerable, and just because one person has purified his wrongdoings, veils, and habitual tendencies does not mean that everyone else has purified theirs. Ultimately, everybody has to travel the path themselves and purify their own obscurations. The buddhas of the past were not able to liberate all sentient beings, not even Avalokiteshvara. But, if one does attain enlightenment, through the power of one's compassion and vast aspirations, one will slowly be able to guide an incredible number of sentient beings toward enlightenment. In particular, when a practitioner attains the rainbow body it is said that 3,000 sentient beings attain liberation simultaneously with the manifestation of the rainbow body.

There are a few cases in the past where many people attained enlightenment simultaneously because they already had the karmic continuity of former practice. In the country of Uddiyana 100,000 people simultaneously achieved enlightenment. But these cases are very rare.

There is no other way to reach enlightenment than by recognizing buddha nature and attaining stability in it. Buddhas of the past did that, and the present-day practitioners who will be the buddhas of the future will do so by recognizing their own nature and attaining stability in it. There is no other way. Nobody else can accomplish enlightenment for us or pull us into liberation. It is completely up to ourselves.

For example, if there were a group in which everybody received the pointing-out instruction, recognized the nature of mind, exerted themselves diligently in practice, and grew accustomed to the buddha nature, certainly the whole group could attain enlightenment within this very lifetime. But people have different capacities and different karmic dispositions, so it is never one hundred percent certain how many actually recognize the buddha nature in the correct way upon having it pointed out. Nor is it ever fixed how many will truly exert themselves in practice after having recognized the buddha nature. For this reason, it is not one hundred percent guaranteed that everybody will accomplish enlightenment in one lifetime.

There have been an incredible number of practitioners in the past who attained accomplishment and liberation, the great bodhisattvas and mahasiddhas of India as well as the Tibetans of different lineages. Just read the life stories of how many practitioners did so; they are like the stars we can see in the night sky. Definitely it is possible—but it is in our own hands.

For sentient beings as a whole, samsara is endless. But for each individual person who practices and awakens to enlightenment there is an end to samsaric existence. There are two possibilities: the endless path of samsara, and the path with an end to samsara. Right now we have the choice between the two. We can practice, gain accomplishment and attain enlightenment, cutting all ties to our existence in samsara as deluded sentient beings. For the person completely under the power of discursive thinking, the path of samsara continues endlessly. When one gains mastery over the essence of mind by perfecting one's practice of *rigpa*, samsaric existence is brought to an end.

Three key words summarize all Dharma teachings: ground, path, and fruition. The ground, the buddhanature, the dharmakaya of all the buddhas, is like a wish-fulfilling jewel. It is the basis for buddhas and sentient beings; there is no difference whatsoever. It is said that the nature of mind is like a wish-fulfilling jewel. Those who fail to recognize this are known as sentient beings; those who realize it are known as buddhas. In other words, the jewel of the buddhas did not fall in the mud, whereas the jewel of sentient beings fell in the mud and was covered by dirt. First there was a jewel, it fell in the mud, under the power of delusion.

Being under the power of delusion or confusion is known as the path. All the attempts to clean the jewel in order to remove the dirt obscuring it are the example for spiritual practices that enable one to gain realization.

The term 'buddha' refers to someone who has realized the ground to begin with. In this context, buddha refers to primordial enlightenment. Sentient beings have no chance for primordial enlightenment since they already have soiled their jewel. But, by cleaning the jewel through engaging in the practices of visualization, recitation, and meditation, one purifies the obscurations of body, speech, and mind and gathers the accumulations of merit and wisdom. Thus there is the possibility to become re-enlightened and that is known as fruition.

Put another way, buddhas do not stray onto the deluded state of a path. Because their jewel is not dropped in the mud, it does not have to be cleaned. The state of sentient beings is like a jewel that fell in the mud. The dirt has to be removed in order to re-establish the purity of the jewel. The story of the wish-fulfilling jewel is that once it is cleaned it can be placed on top of a victory banner. One can make offerings to it and it will then fulfill all wishes—that is the fruition.

The ground is the buddha nature, which is like a wish-fulfilling jewel. It is present in all beings just like oil is present in any sesame seed. All beings have buddha nature, but this alone is not enough. The second thing needed is the support of a physical body, the precious human body. It is only as a human that one is able to practice and awaken to enlightenment. Insects and animals do have an enlightened essence, but their body is not a support for realizing it because they cannot receive teachings or speak—they don't come to Dharma talks and receive teachings. Only humans do this. The third factor needed is the positive circumstance of a spiritual teacher. These three need to coincide: having buddha nature; being a human possessing a precious human body, and connecting with a spiritual teacher. Then it's possible to receive the pith instructions on how to recognize and realize the nature that we already have. Although we cannot be primordially enlightened, we can become re-enlightened.

We presently possess all three of these factors: we have the buddha nature, we are humans, and we are connected to a spiritual teacher. If we let this precious opportunity slip away, don't practice, and just watch life pass by until we die, that would be like returning empty-handed from an island full of jewels. Sentient beings are lost; we've lost our buddha-nature. An example for this is a stupid person who loses himself in a crowd of people and doesn't know who he is until someone tells him, "Here you are!" If we don't recognize our true nature we are like the stupid person lost in a crowd, asking "Where am I?" We need to find ourselves. Even though we seem to be lost, by virtue of the positive circumstance of the spiritual teacher we can be introduced to our lost nature. The spiritual teacher doesn't hand us something we don't already possess. We have it, and yet we have lost it, so to speak. There is no greater misfortune than losing what we already have, the buddha within ourselves. The qualities of an enlightened buddha are not *his* qualities; they are the qualities of the buddha-nature fully manifest. We also possess that same potential, but it is hidden, lying dormant.

If our buddha nature is beyond delusion and liberation, can't we also say that we are in essence primordially enlightened? We could possibly succeed in convincing ourselves with such a philosophical trick, but it's not really true, because we have already strayed onto the path. If we had never fallen into confusion, we could rightfully claim to be primordially enlightened. But unfortunately it is too late to make that claim. Our precious wish-fulfilling jewel has already fallen into the stinking mud.

Primordial enlightenment means that ground and fruition are identical and there is no path of delusion to be cleared away. This is definitely different from the situation of we who have already strayed onto the path and therefore need to clear away delusion in order to reach fruition. Take the example of a myriad of jewels: some are covered with mud, some are clean. All of them are jewels, but each is distinctly individual. Sentient beings' minds cognize individually so we have to say that they are separate.

This is quite a good example, to view all beings and buddhas as countless jewels, some covered with dirt, some clean. They are not identical even though they have the same qualities. If the minds of all sentient beings were one, then when one individual attains enlightenment, everybody else would be liberated at the same moment. But if you attain enlightenment it doesn't mean that I will be enlightened. Understand it this way: although beings have similar qualities, we are not one. We have the same essence, which is empty and cognizant, but our form of manifestation is separate, distinct from that of another sentient being.

If I recognize buddha nature and attain enlightenment it doesn't mean that another person also recognizes and attains enlightenment. Sorry about that! If beings shared both the same essence and manifestation, when one reached enlightenment everyone else would too. We are like pure gold scattered in different places: equal quality, but separate pieces. Likewise with water: the properties of water are identical, but there is water in many diverse locations in this world. Or think of the space inside our different houses—the same space but with various shapes. The empty cognizance is identical, but the 'form' around it is distinctly individual. Some jewels were lucky. Some fell in the mud.

IMPERMANENCE

The world outside is fleeting, as are the beings it contains.
Definitely death lies at the end of birth.
The time of death is uncertain,
But when death arrives only the Dharma can help me.
Without wasting time I will endeavor one-pointedly in practice.

Karmey Khenpo Rinchen Dargye

Whether we are beginners or not, we should know that nothing in this world lasts. To understand this fully and to really take it to heart is the foundation of all Buddhist practice. Not taking impermanence to heart prevents our Dharma practice from being successful. The starting point, the first step through the door to Dharma practice, is the understanding that life is impermanent, that our time is running out.

We believe that what we have will last for some time, but no matter where we look in this world, we find nothing that is stable or permanent. As soon as the sun and moon rise, moment by moment they draw closer to setting. They don't linger in between for even an instant. Seasons change, the days, months, and years pass by. The whole universe is in flux as it goes through the stages of formation, subsistence, disintegration, and disappearance. All living things perpetually change. Life is like a candle that slowly burns down, getting shorter, not longer. Life doesn't wait; it is like a waterfall that is continuously running, never stopping. Every moment we are drawing closer to death. We probably understand this intellectually, but it's very important to think carefully about it so that it remains vividly present in our mind.

Not really taking impermanence to heart, we make long-term plans and take them seriously. Consider yesterday, today, and tomorrow. Yesterday will never come back; it is part of our life that is gone. Past moments, hours, and days never return. Tomorrow becomes today and today fades into yesterday. When today has become yesterday, nobody in the whole world can bring it back to the present. Our life passes, and the fact that it can end at any moment means we are in a most precarious and dangerous situation.

We can be certain that not a single person alive now will be alive 150 years from now. Nevertheless, nobody believes he will eventually die. We are always preoccupied with plans to create and establish something that can be continued, maybe not just for ourselves, but for our children and grandchildren.

If we could just live forever in this present body, we wouldn't have to worry about any aftermath. But death is unavoidable. No one is immortal. Each and every one of us must someday die. We are like a tree that appears to be growing but is decaying inside. Sooner or later the rot takes over and the tree falls.

Undeniably, our present life will end in death. The time before death is more comfortable than what follows. No matter how bad our situation may be while we are alive, we can always try to improve it through our ingenuity. At this time we have free will and the opportunity to change our circumstances. But the events that occur after death depend totally on our personal karma. We are absolutely powerless and choiceless regarding the experiences that will arise.

After death, depending on the karma accumulated by our past actions, we are thrust into a new existence. If we desire rebirth in a good situation, we should realize that the causes for this are currently in our own hands. What can be of help after death? Only the Dharma practice that we invest our time in right now can ensure positive future circumstances. Nothing else will be of any benefit; we can't rely on anything else.

In Buddhist training, revulsion and renunciation are known as the "two feet of meditation practice." Revulsion is losing our appetite for samsaric existence and realizing that samsaric pursuits are futile and pointless, and do not yield any permanent pleasure and happiness whatsoever. Renunciation means to understand that time is running out and everything passes.

Revulsion is the feeling people suffering from jaundice or liver disease experience when served fried food; they are either very nauseous or they vomit. In the same way, when we realize that all the achievements of the six realms of samsara are futile, insubstantial, and meaningless, we lose our appetite for them.

Renunciation, wanting to be free from samsara, is to realize that all conditioned samsaric states are painful and everything is impermanent. We need to acknowledge sincerely and honestly that our life is a fleeting, fragile existence. Our present body is as perishable as a rainbow in the sky, our breath is like mist on the mountains, and all our thoughts and feelings are like bubbles that appear one moment and vanish the next. From the core of our heart, we need to have this conviction.

Worldly people are only interested in having nice clothes to wear, getting good food to eat, and securing a good reputation. But food, clothing, and a good name are very unstable achievements. In fact, although we really only need enough clothes to keep warm and not freeze, somehow we feel the minimum is not enough. We don't just want ordinary clothes: we want special, fashionable, designer clothes. Regarding food, we only need to eat so that the body survives and doesn't starve. However, mere sustenance doesn't really satisfy us. We want something extraordinary to eat, gourmet food. We also want to be sure to have all the necessities of life when we grow old. We constantly worry about the future, stashing our money away for our old age. When we die, if we have always dressed nicely we will leave behind a well-dressed corpse. If we only wore ordinary clothes, we leave a corpse in ordinary clothing. But a corpse is a corpse, and the attire doesn't make any real difference. We can't take our clothes, supply of food or bank account with us.

Of these three, food, clothing, and reputation, the worst is craving a good name and respect. When one moves in lower social circles, one longs for the prestige of being talented, influential, clever, or beautiful. One wants to be regarded as somebody. When one circulates among kings and ministers in the highest ranks of society, one desires world fame. The need for a good name is even more pointless than the other two because at least one can eat the food and wear the clothes. One can't really do anything with reputation; it's like thunder in the sky or an echo that vanishes the moment after resounding.

Our reputation is totally useless. When we die, even if we have been the king of a great nation, although those still alive will say, "Oh, our king died" in the bardo state we won't be greeted by any official welcoming party. The terrifying figures appearing in the bardo, the Lord of Death and his henchmen, do not respect anyone, regardless of his or her social standing. On the contrary, the more we indulge in superficial self-esteem in this life, that much more loss will we reap in the bardo state. At that time there will be nothing whatsoever left to support such a conviction. Practitioners regard the craving for food, clothing, and reputation as detrimental. They curtail their preoccupation with these things and are satisfied with the bare necessities of life.

Until now, we have had so many past lives, one after the other. There are no immortals in this world; everyone dies. After death we will be reborn among one of the six classes of beings, remain there for some time, then die once again to be reborn elsewhere. On and on it goes, through countless future lives. This chain of birth, death, rebirth, and death again is powered by our karmic deeds and their fruition. This whole cycle is known as samsara, which means 'spinning' or 'circling' like a cog in a machine.

That which decides where we will be reborn is our karmic debt. If we have committed many positive karmic deeds, the effect is that we are reborn in one of the three higher realms of samsara. If, on the contrary, we have committed many negative actions the karmic effect will be rebirth in one of the three lower realms of samsara. The three higher realms are the realms of human beings, demigods, and gods. An even higher achievement is liberation from samsara, which refers to rebirth in one of the buddhafields. Higher than even liberation is buddhahood, complete enlightenment itself.

In accordance with the severity of one's negative karma, one could take rebirth in one of the three lower realms, as an animal or, if the karmic misdeeds are even worse, as a hungry ghost or a hell being in one of the hot or cold hells. All of these realms are created by our own karmic actions. The one who knew that our good and evil actions have an effect and that there are higher and lower realms was the perfectly Awakened One, the Buddha.

The Buddha named the world we are born into *Saha*, which means 'indiscernible,' that which cannot be seen clearly. If we do an evil action, its effect does not appear immediately. When we do something good that result is not evident to anybody. If the result of a negative action would ripen the moment after enacting it, nobody would commit evil. Likewise, people would not hold back from positive deeds because the effect would be instantaneous. However, the results of actions do not ripen immediately; they are not instantly discernible, but only ripen slowly. Due to not realizing the positive and negative results of actions and not understanding impermanence, we are completely oblivious to the consequences of our actions. We don't see what is happening, we don't see the result of our actions, we don't see how much or how little merit we have, so we walk around like stupid cows. If the effect of an action were to manifest immediately, then even if someone said "Please do a negative action," there is no way we would do so because we would instantly see the result. If we have eyes and stand on the brink of an abyss we will not jump, because we see that by jumping we would die. If we could see the effect of our good and evil actions, we would never commit negative actions. But this world is not like that: here, the results of actions appear unclear and vague.

If the effect of an action could be immediately discerned, we would not need a teacher to act as a substitute for the Buddha and tell us to be careful, do good, and avoid evil actions. What is right and wrong would be self-evident. But because we are in a world where the effects of actions are not self-evident, it is important to listen to a teacher repeating what the Buddha said. He repeats words that are not lies, such as good actions give good results, negative actions give negative results. But it's not enough just to hear that. We need to believe it as well, because unless we trust what has been said, we won't act in accordance with it. Some people think that when a Buddhist teacher says something like "good actions lead to good results" that he is lying or doesn't know what he's talking about. It's important to trust because we ourselves cannot see clearly. Due to ignorance we don't see the effect of our positive or negative actions. We don't know what we did in the past or if we will die tomorrow.

The Buddhist teachings were given by the Buddha Shakyamuni, who could see the past, present, and future as clearly as something placed in his own hand. He gave teachings on how to act as a legacy to future generations. He said there are buddhafields, there are lower realms, there is karma, the cause and effect of actions. Normal people can't see clearly, so to help them he told them things like, "Avoid negative actions, they will bring negative results; do what is correct and positive, it will bring positive results." He also told us that this life is not the only one; that there are future lives, there were past lives. The Buddha was extremely kind. In between the time the Buddha lived and now there have been people who followed his teachings, not only the teachings on how to behave, but also the more subtle teachings. They attained special results: some could fly through the sky and pass through solid rock; some died without leaving a physical body, and became rainbow light. It is not only because I am Buddhist that I believe the Buddha. It is because there have been so many since him who showed very special signs of accomplishment. That is why I feel I can safely believe all his words.

Because the teacher was so great, Buddhism became widespread in many countries, including Tibet. Apart from Buddhism, Tibetans don't know much. They don't know how to make airplanes, cars, or other technical wonders. But mundane things bring only superficial benefit and lack ultimate value. Instead of making outer machinery, Tibetans focused on spiritual machinery. Many attained the rainbow body. There was the great master Karmapa who defeated the four demons, the first Karmapa, Düsum Khyenpa. There is one praise to him which says, "Victor over the four demons, knower of the three times, Düsum Khyenpa." In short, it's very important to have trust in the Buddha's teachings if one wishes to apply them. If one tries to apply them without trust they won't help much.

So what is truly meaningful in this life? Only the pursuance of buddhahood, the state of complete enlightenment. The Three Jewels are truly meaningful: the Precious Buddha, his teachings, known as the Precious Dharma, and those who explain the teachings and keep the tradition alive through practice, the Precious Sangha. From the core of our heart, we should place our trust and confidence in these three. When we genuinely feel from deep within there is nothing more precious and valuable than the Three Jewels, this is known as taking refuge. These three Precious Ones will never deceive us or abuse our trust in this life, at the moment of death, in the bardo state, or in our following lives.

How is everything perceived in the state of complete enlightenment? Imagine a crystal ball in your hand: the ball does not obstruct anything, but is completely transparent. Everything all around can be seen simultaneously in the crystal ball, and is vividly clear. In the same way, the enlightened state perceives everything in all directions at the same moment and in a completely unobstructed fashion. The Dharma teachings are an expression arising from this state, and are totally free from any falsehood or pretense.

There was not just one buddha. In the past there have been countless awakened ones. In the present world eon, one thousand buddhas will appear. In future eons, a countless number of buddhas will appear. When a fully enlightened one appears and teaches, the words he utters, which are totally free of any deception, are the Precious Dharma. Those who uphold those teachings and pass them on to others are the Precious Sangha. In this world, we can find nothing more valuable than the Buddha, Dharma, and Sangha.

The Dharma teachings given by the Enlightened One would be nothing more than writing on paper without someone to uphold and propagate them. Those who uphold the teachings one after another, like the holders of a family line, are the Precious Sangha. Without great bodhisattvas and masters to teach others, there would be no living tradition. Throughout the centuries these beings have given many commentaries clarifying the Buddha's words, so that today many hundreds of volumes of these books can be found. The Precious Sangha is made up of the teachers and masters who can explain what the Dharma teachings mean and how we can implement them. We need living beings who can communicate the profundity of the Dharma.

The spiritual blessings of the Buddha, Dharma, and Sangha are not far away. The sun in the sky is quite distant, but the moment we hold a mirror up to it, a reflection of the sun immediately appears. In the same way, the very moment we feel faith and devotion, the blessings of the Buddha, Dharma, and Sangha are with us. These blessings are said to be like a hook, while the openness that occurs in the moment of faith is compared to a ring. The hook catches the ring, just as faith and devotion open us fully to the blessings.

To strengthen their connection to the Buddha, Dharma, and Sangha, a great number of people have relied on three unmistaken qualities: the unmistaken quality of the Buddha's words, the unmistaken quality of the statements of noble beings and the enlightened masters, and the unmistaken quality of their own root guru's oral instructions which they put into practice. By combining these unmistaken qualities with their own experience, innumerable people have been able to reach a state totally free from doubt. Moreover, they attained great accomplishments so they could fly through the sky, pass freely through solid rock, and, without leaving a physical body behind, go to the celestial realms at the time of death. Some could travel to distant places without leaving their bodies. For example, at the time of the first Karmapa, several Indian panditas came to Tibet. After meeting the Karmapa, they told others, "We know this old guy with the monkey face very well. He came to India many times and participated in the feast offerings with our guru. We have met him many times before in India." In fact, the Karmapa had never been known to leave Tibet, but a great master like him had the ability to fly off to visit a faraway feast offering and return at his leisure.

By combining the unmistaken qualities with our own experience, we can reach a state totally free from doubt. It's not like we are told, "Don't doubt! Just believe!" It's not like that. It is possible to be completely free from doubt through these three unmistaken qualities. Countless practitioners have achieved that. I myself have no doubt whatsoever in the words of the Buddha.

There are past lives and future lives; there are definite effects from good and evil actions; there are higher realms above and lower realms below. The reason I feel certain of these things is the unmistaken qualities mentioned above. If I were only to rely on myself, I would be unable to reach this certainty because I have never visited the higher realms or been to the hells, nor can I perceive past or future lives. Therefore I do not rely solely on my own judgment. The reason I am able to appear so confident is because I use these unmistaken qualities as confirmation.

What is really valuable? Our precious human rebirth, this body, given to us by our father and mother. We have all our senses intact, we are intelligent and capable of understanding—it is an incredible advantage, like a wish-fulfilling jewel. Another analogy compares being endowed with a precious human rebirth to arriving on an island where jewels abound. As this is the case, it's extremely important not to stand around with our hands in our pockets or folded across our chest. This life should be put to use and be taken full advantage of, so that we don't return empty-handed.

Right now, because we possess a human rebirth, we are clever, practical-minded, and able to carry out most of our intentions. But what if we were animals living in a forest or on a mountaintop? What would be our ability to determine our own future? We would be unable to receive teachings and put them into practice. Right now, we do possess the precious human body and have the power and opportunity to practice the Dharma. Definitely we should do so.

Right now we are at a crossroads where we can go either up or down. Going down requires no effort on our part; it is easily accomplished because it is our natural tendency to continue old patterns of negative emotions. Dharma practice, on the other hand, requires effort; it needs to be cultivated. It is like trying to roll a great boulder uphill. It won't arrive there on its own, it must be pushed up. If we let it go, it will roll all the way downhill under its own power. We don't need to help it. In the same way, we don't have to put much effort into accomplishing negative actions; they come about automatically because it is our natural tendency. Practicing virtue and avoiding negativity is what requires effort.

The Buddha spoke of the ultimate view that cuts through the root of the three poisons. If we want to bring an end to samsaric existence and cross the ocean of samsaric pain and suffering, we need to practice the Precious Dharma that the Buddha taught. If, on the other hand, we are happy and content to continue in the three realms of samsara and we are not tired of undergoing endless suffering, of course we don't need to practice the Dharma. If we think, "I've been circling around taking birth, growing old, getting sick, and dying, taking birth, growing old, getting sick, and dying again and again endlessly, and I'll just go on like that," we can certainly continue doing so, and we don't need to practice the Dharma. When we end up as an ox or cow, we just have to eat grass, fall asleep, wake up, and abide in stupidity until we are slaughtered and eaten. Samsaric existence does not require our efforts in order to perpetuate itself. It will continue automatically. In the chant known as the *Lamenting Apology of Rudra*, a line says, "In the past, I have cried enough tears to fill an ocean. The bones of my past skeletons, if heaped together, would be higher than the world's tallest mountain."

To put it bluntly, if we want happiness we need to engage in Dharma practice, but if we are satisfied with pain and suffering we needn't bother practicing. While driving, when we reach a fork in the road where we can go either right or left, it is our own hands that will steer right or left; the choice is ours. In the same way, whether we want to steer a course that will bring happiness in the future or continue on a course that brings us endless pain is entirely up to ourselves. No one else can steer for us. But if we can turn towards enlightenment and attain buddhahood, at that point we will be able to benefit not just ourselves but countless other sentient beings.

Another word for buddha is *sugata*, meaning 'having gone to bliss', to a place where not even the word 'suffering' is heard. Happy in this life, happy at the time of death, happy in the bardo state, and happy in the future lives is one way to travel. On the other hand, samsaric existence is painful now with the suffering of illness, and later with the experience of death and the confusion of the bardo state that leads us into the lower realms where we experience even more suffering. Samsara only goes from bad to worse.

An advanced practitioner will be happy even when facing illness or at the moment of death. He will be joyful at the prospect of dying because he knows that what comes after will only be better and better. A good practitioner is confident enough to be joyful during sickness and joyful at the moment of death, whereas an ordinary person is depressed by illness and desperate at the moment of death. When he must leave behind his relatives, children, and possessions, he suffers tremendously. All the nice things he worked so hard to acquire will now be carried off and enjoyed by others—truly, how sad.

In Tibet there's a saying, "When seen from afar, yaks look healthy and handsome; close up, they look like sickly sheep; but under the fleece, they are infested with lice and scabies." In other words, when we look at others from afar they may appear to have happiness, prestige, friends, and wealth. But when we get closer we see that they are not really very happy and their situation is not so ideal. There is always something to complain about, and when we get very close and examine their inner feelings, each person has his own set of worries and carries his own burden around with him. No one is in perfect happiness. That's why the Buddha called samsara an ocean of suffering, not an ocean of bliss. But I don't need to convince you of this; you can understand it from your own experience.

Don't just take my word for it, but decide for yourselves what is really meaningful to pursue in this life. I am only trying to refresh your memory and clarify what you already know very well. Nonetheless, appearances, what we smell, hear, see, taste, and touch, are seductive. If we allow ourselves to be carried away by our fickle mind, even though we may really want to practice the Dharma, it is somehow postponed. We think, "Well, if not today, I can practice tomorrow or maybe next month, or next year." Or never. Things don't occur exactly in accordance with our plans. It is said, "When I was young, I was controlled by others and couldn't practice the Dharma. When I grew up, I played around and couldn't practice the Dharma. Now, I'm old and too weak to practice the Dharma. Alas, alas! What shall I do?" Decide for yourselves: are you able to practice the Dharma?

If we apply the teachings, the first beneficiary will be ourselves. Later, after we have taken care of ourselves, we will be capable of helping countless other beings. On the other hand, if we don't succeed in benefiting ourselves and others through Dharma practice, we are not really adding more beings to the ocean of samsara, but only adding ourselves to the multitudes already roaming through the lower realms. That is not of such great benefit. Wouldn't it be better to attain enlightenment and leave samsara behind, rather than just adding ourselves to the countless beings suffering in the lower realms?

THE INNERMOST
REFUGE

Namo
In the empty essence, dharmakaya,
In the cognizant nature, sambhogakaya,
In the manifold capacity, nirmanakaya,
I take refuge until enlightenment.

Padmasambhava

Certain concepts in Buddhism are similar to the Western concept of an omniscient, omnipotent god. The closest thing to this divinity is the three kayas: dharmakaya, sambhogakaya and nirmanakaya. Although we could call these three kayas "God," that is not really necessary. I will now explain what these three kayas are.

The first, dharmakaya, is all-pervasive like space; in actuality it is the unmistaken nature of our mind. Sambhogakaya is like the light of the sun, and is the cognizant quality of mind. Nirmanakaya is like the appearance of a rainbow in space, and acts for the welfare of all beings. Outwardly we can think of the three kayas as space, sunlight, and a rainbow, but the meaning of these symbols lies within our own mind.

The Dharma teachings are structured as two aspects: means and knowledge, known in Sanskrit as *upaya* and *prajna*. The aspect of means is to visualize the buddhas in front of oneself and engage in different practices. The knowledge aspect is to realize that the buddhas are contained within our buddha nature, the essence of our mind. The reason it is possible for us to reach enlightenment is because the enlightened essence is already present in ourselves. The real buddha is the nature of our mind, the knowledge aspect.

This in itself, however, is not enough, because the buddha nature is covered by veils. In order to remove the veils we need the means, which provides a way to purify the obscurations and gather the two accumulations of merit and wisdom. A practice in which we think that the Buddha is outside ourselves, ignoring the buddha within, will by itself never bring complete enlightenment. If we expect the Buddha up there in the sky to give us all the common and supreme accomplishments, we are placing our hopes in an object external to ourselves. The ultimate deity is within our own mind. We attain enlightenment by recognizing our true nature and training in that recognition.

All Dharma teachings have two aspects: the relative or superficial and the ultimate or real. Visualizing the Buddha as being outside ourselves is superficial, and is not enough for enlightenment. The basis for awakening to enlightenment is to experience the buddha in ourselves. But the recognition of the real is nevertheless dependent upon the superficial, because it is by making offerings, purifying obscurations, and gathering the accumulations with the support of a buddha imagined outside that we can remove the veils and realize the buddha within.

Taking refuge means to place our trust in the Buddha, the teacher. What he taught is known as the Dharma, and the great practitioners who have followed those teachings are called the Sangha. If we look at ourselves right now, we can see that alone we lack the power to reach enlightenment. By placing our trust in the Three Jewels we receive blessings, which make it easier to realize accomplishment. But understand that the true basis for awakening to the state of enlightenment is found within ourselves.

This potential for enlightenment is present as the nature of our own mind. To recognize that fact is the knowledge aspect. Then, in order to fully facilitate this recognition we apply the means—visualizing the Buddha, making praises, and performing different types of conceptual practices. The true path of the buddhas is the unity of means and knowledge. It is not sufficient to simply apply the means, thinking that a superior being is outside oneself and making offerings and praises to that outer image. Only by combining the two aspects of means and knowledge do we attain enlightenment.

An ordinary example for the unity of means and knowledge is to bring together a person who knows how to make an airplane, the knowledge aspect, with the all the materials for the airplane, the means. Having all the pieces of an airplane in itself is not enough. Neither is only having somebody who knows how to make one. It is only by combining the two that a plane that will actually fly can be made.

According to Vajrayana, one combines the means as the development stage with the knowledge aspect as the completion stage. The development stage entails visualization—creating the image of the divine being—praises, confessions, offerings, and the other sections of the sadhana practice. The completion stage involves recognizing the nature of mind by looking into *who* visualizes, thus bringing the buddha nature into practical experience. The development stage is necessary because right now we are normal beings, and a normal being is unenlightened, unstable in the realization of the buddha nature. By ourselves we do not have complete power, so we ask for help from the buddhas and bodhisattvas. By offering the seven branches, for instance, we purify our obscurations, removing that which prevents us from gaining true insight. The knowledge aspect is the nature of our mind. Both means and knowledge are necessary. Each aids the other. Only utilizing the method is like gathering the husk without getting the corn cob—it is not enough.

Another example is when a person studies to become a Tibetan doctor. He starts with the knowledge aspect, learning how to identify different parts of the body, to diagnose diseases, what medicines to apply for a successful cure, and so forth. However, knowledge by itself is not sufficient to cure anybody; the doctor also needs the necessary medicines. So collecting the medicinal plants and blending the right concoctions is the means aspect. It is the combination of these two aspects, means and knowledge, that cures a sick person.

The equivalent of a god or supreme being in Buddhism is Samantabhadra, or in English the Ever-Excellent, who is the primordial dharmakaya buddha. When

Samantabhadra manifests on the sambhogakaya level he is known as Vajradhara, the Vajra Holder. His nirmana-kaya form is Vajrasattva. There are an incredible number of gods and deities in Buddhism, but their basic source, where they manifest from, is the dharmakaya buddha Samantabhadra, the sambhogakaya buddha Vajradhara and the nirmanakaya buddha Vajrasattva. Deities are not related to one another like a family relationship, with some being parents and others the offspring. Their body is self-existing, while their mind is pure wisdom, innate wakefulness.

The self-existing body of dharmakaya is like space, totally beyond any constructs or concepts. The body of sambhogakaya is like rainbow light. The nirmanakaya manifests on a physical level in this world without de-parting from the state of the other two. One thousand nirmanakaya buddhas will appear during this world's present period, which is known as the Good Eon. Bud-dha Shakyamuni is the fourth of these one thousand. The nirmanakaya buddhas are first emanated and then re-absorbed. In the instance of Buddha Shakyamuni there were one billion emanations, meaning one billion simultaneous Buddha Sakyamunis in different realms.

Everything appears out of the dharmakaya, out of Buddha Samantabhadra. The sambhogakaya itself is manifest from dharmakaya and is represented by the five buddha families. Out of sambhogakaya appear nirmana-kayas, beings who manifest in order to benefit others. To benefit human beings, a buddha must appear in human form; therefore, the thousand buddhas of this eon are human beings. Unless buddhas appear as human beings, how can we see them and receive teachings? We don't perceive the sambhogakaya level and, needless to say, ordinary people do not perceive the dharmakaya level either. Nirmanakayas appear as teachers in flesh-and-blood form, just like Buddha Shakyamuni. These beings communicate the teachings, the Buddhadharma. Since people have different capacities, there are three or nine different levels of teachings, generally known as the nine vehicles.

These teachers are also known as the tamers, while the various classes of beings—hell beings, hungry ghosts, animals, human beings, demi-gods and gods—are those to be tamed. Those who tame them are the emanations of the buddhas that appear in each of the six realms. A buddha is someone who has accomplished everything there is to accomplish for the benefit of himself. All his activity is aimed at accomplishing the welfare of others. A buddha appears only for others.

The buddhas manifest in all the six realms, not just the human world. In the realm of gods the Buddha is known as Shakra, the king of gods. Among the demigods he is Taksang, among humans he is Shakyamuni, among animals he is Steadfast Lion, among the hungry ghosts he is Flaming Mouth, and among the hell-beings he is Dharmaraja. Most beings only perceive these bud-dha emanations as kings or rulers of their various realms.

Nirmanakayas appear in four different ways. Cre-ated nirmanakayas are sacred images, like the three famous statues that were originally kept at the Bodhgaya stupa, two of which are now in Lhasa. Then there is the supreme nirmanakaya, which, according to the sutras, is the Buddha Shakyamuni. The supreme Nirmanakaya for the Vajrayana teachings is Padmasambhava, who manifested as one billion simultaneous Padmasambha-vas. There are also the incarnated nirmanakayas, the great masters who in the Tibetan tradition are known as *tulkus*. Finally there are the variegated nirmanakayas, which appear in many different forms in order to influ-ence or benefit beings according to their needs. These can appear in an incredible variety of forms, including bridges or ships. Buddhas can appear in every possible form, in a way that lies far beyond the domain of ordi-nary people.

Now I will explain the relationship between the three kayas. The dharmakaya is like space in that it accommodates the manifestations of the other two kayas. Space is all-encompassing: nothing appears or disappears outside of it, everything manifests and eventually disintegrates within infinite space. The sambhogakaya is like the sun, which appears in the sky and shines with unchanging brilliance. And the nirmanakaya is like the surface of water, which reflects the sun. One sun can simultaneously be reflected upon billions of surfaces of water; wherever there is water the reflection of the sun appears.

Nirmanakaya manifests in all different ways, including the supreme, created, incarnated, and variegated nirmanakayas, without leaving dharmakaya and sambhogakaya, and in accordance with what is required to benefit beings. *Nirmana* means magically created, like a magical apparition. Those who have total mastery over life and death are not like we normal people, who cannot voluntarily leave and enter incarnations. Our rebirth is decided by the force of our karmic actions, but nirmanakayas are not bound by the law of karma. They are like a reflection of the sun. The sambhogakaya, which is like the sun shining in the sky, cannot appear outside space or without space; the two cannot be separated. Similarly, the sun's reflection on the surface of water cannot appear without the sun. Although we give the three kayas three different names, they are in essence indivisible. This indivisibility of the three kayas is sometimes known as the essence-kaya, the fourth kaya, which is the nature of our mind. The dharmakaya, sambhogakaya, and nirmana-kaya depicted as being outside are merely symbols. What they refer to, the true meaning, is the nature of our own mind.

DEVOTION AND COMPASSION

The play of overwhelming compassion being unobstructed,
In the moment of love the empty essence nakedly dawns.
May we constantly practice, day and night,
This supreme path of unity, devoid of errors.

Lord Karmapa Rangjung Dorje

The most perfect circumstance for realizing the correct view of emptiness is upwardly to generate devotion to all the enlightened ones and downwardly to cultivate compassion for all sentient beings. This is mentioned in *The Aspiration of Mahamudra* by the third Karmapa, Rangjung Dorje. This incredibly profound song of realization expounds teachings on the ground, path, and fruition, as well as all the key points for Mahamudra,

Dzogchen, and Madhyamika. One of the lines is "In the moment of love the empty essence nakedly dawns." Here "love" should be understood as both devotion and compassion. In the moment of devotion we bring to mind the eminence of our master and lineage gurus, doing this sincerely, not just superficially. One thinks of their great qualities with such genuine admiration and devotion that the hairs of one's body stand on end and one's eyes are filled with tears. This heart-felt appreciation should be genuine, because it is only through the kindness of the guru that the mind essence can possibly be understood. From this gratitude, strong devotion is felt, stripping our minds bare. That very moment, we unmistakenly and unerringly recognize the natural face of rigpa.

It is the same way when thinking with compassion of all sentient beings. Although they possess self-existing wisdom they are unaware of it, remaining completely deluded life after life. Chasing after samsara's illusory experiences, they undergo tremendous suffering. It is not like we, as Buddhist practitioners, have an enlightened essence of rigpa and they don't. Everybody is totally equal; yet, not knowing their own nature, sentient beings suffer incessantly. Thinking in this way, one is overcome with great pity and compassion. At that instant of true compassion, as in the moment of true devotion, the empty essence dawns nakedly.

In the Kagyü and Nyingma traditions it is said that devotion is the universal panacea, the medicine that can cure all sicknesses. If one just focuses on devotion one does not need to spend years studying debate, philosophy, grammar, art and so forth. In the past, thousands of practitioners attained accomplishment through the path of devotion combined with the paths of Mahamudra and Dzogchen. To ignore compassion, devotion, and renunciation is like a bird trying to fly without wings: it's not possible. One should remember the famous statement: 'Devotion is the head of meditation, revulsion is the foot of meditation and nondistraction is the heart of meditation.' To take a similar example, consider a person: if we call the view of emptiness the heart, devotion the head, and compassion the feet, how can he travel anywhere using only the heart of emptiness? How can he walk without legs?

Devotion and compassion are not mentioned here simply because we ought to feel them, There is a direct reason for cultivating them. The teachings mention that compassion and devotion should be unfabricated, but this doesn't happen automatically in the beginning. We need to cultivate them, to use some effort to produce these feelings. In other words, in the beginning, we must rely on conceptual thought to make it possible to have compassion and devotion.

Think of it this way: we wouldn't know any Dharma teachings or how to attain liberation if it weren't for the buddhas, their teachings, and their perfect followers. The buddhas are not like oneself; they have great qualities. Bringing this to mind naturally and unavoidably generates devotion. Similarly, to generate compassion, think of how it is a fact that all sentient beings have been our own parents. In that sense they are closely related to us. If we really think of how other beings suffer, what they go through, we cannot help but feel compassion. When we think of their suffering there is a real reason for pity.

Having slowly cultivated devotion and compassion, we can use them as an aid to genuinely recognize rigpa. Gradually, the sequence is reversed. The natural quality of recognizing the naked state of rigpa is an unfabricated devotion and compassion that doesn't need to be mustered.

Devotion and compassion are enhancements to the practice of emptiness, of the view. Once all misdeeds and veils are purified through conditioned virtue, the unconditioned virtue increases. At first devotion and compassion are necessary to create. They are important stepping stones to recognizing rigpa. Unfabricated and natural devotion and compassion are the expression of rigpa, but not for a beginner. In the context of Dzogchen, it is said that compassion and devotion naturally occur, without any effort. But frankly speaking, for a beginner it doesn't happen like that. At first we have to cultivate devotion and compassion, to put some effort into developing them. Later on, as we become more stable in awareness, they become effortless and unfabricated. It is this way in Mahamudra, Dzogchen, and Madhyamika.

The main practice of devotion is taking refuge and the main practice of compassion is to generate bodhichitta. If we investigate, we will not find a single Vajrayana practice without those two, taking refuge and generating bodhichitta. Look at it this way: once we have a heavy investment in taking refuge and generating bodhichitta, we have the capital to be able to do the business of the higher practices and gain the profit of the development stage, the completion stage, and the three great practices—Mahamudra, Dzogchen, and Madhyamika. Without the capital, we won't be able to do any business at all. Devotion and compassion are the basic capital for Buddhist practice.

Unless we connect with the two types of precious bodhichitta, we will not approach enlightenment even in the slightest; this is certain. The two types of bodhichitta are relative bodhichitta, compassion, and ultimate bodhichitta, the insight into emptiness. Without these two, there is absolutely no way to take even one step closer towards buddhahood. Any Dharma practice devoid of these two kinds of bodhichitta will not bring the practitioner even one step towards enlightenment—I will swear to that.

If we want to quickly awaken to buddhahood, it is essential to unite means and knowledge. Whatever conceptual practice we do should ideally be combined with the recognition of mind essence. Devotion and compassion are the heart of conceptual Dharma practice.

The great masters of the Kagyü lineage state that it is delusion to count on any method for recognizing mind essence other than purifying obscurations, gathering the accumulations, and relying on the blessings of a realized master. This means that no matter how smart or strong we are, if we don't follow a master and instead stubbornly push ourselves through years of meditation training without developing compassion and devotion, purifying veils, and gathering the accumulations, we will remain deluded.

The essence of both devotion and compassion is actually the same: it is a kind of love. Whether that feeling is directed towards enlightened pure beings or ordinary impure beings, whether it is devotion or compassion, the essence remains the same: the mind is laid bare of thoughts at the moment the empty essence dawns nakedly, and can be directly perceived. In the Kagyü lineage, devotion is always said to be the main quality to focus on, and so the Kagyü lineage is known as the lineage of devotion. But compassion or devotion are the same in facilitating the realization of mind essence.

To reiterate, our training in devotion, compassion, purifying the obscurations, and gathering the accumulations should be combined with recognizing our mind essence. Otherwise, to reach enlightenment using means without knowledge takes a tremendously long time—three eons, according to the Sutra path. The Vajrayana path is much swifter.

Vajrasattva

Visualize the power of support, Vajrasattva, and proceeded by the power of remorse, the intense feeling of regret and sorrow for evil actions and downfalls committed, practice the antidote, the power of application, the visualization for recitation of the mantra.

Karmey Khenpo

The practice of Vajrayana is said to entail great risk but also great advantage. The example for this is the proverbial snake in the bamboo tube, which can only go up or down; there is no other direction for the snake to go. Likewise, there is only up or down for the practitioner who enters the path of Vajrayana. Vajrayana is not like the lower vehicles where there is not that much risk but also not that much gain.

The snake cannot go right or left in the bamboo tube, only up or down. If one keeps one's samayas well, remaining in awareness, it is certain that in this very body and lifetime, one can reach the level of Unified Vajra Holder, the state of complete enlightenment. If one is unable to keep the sacred commitments of Vajrayana, one will definitely go down, plunging to what is known as the Vajra Hell in Vajrayana or the Hell of Incessant Torment in the Sutra teachings. This is one extreme for a practitioner. The other is to go to the dharmakaya sphere, in Dzogchen this is described as "dissolved but unobscured state of inner brilliance."

Samayas are difficult to keep. It is said that breaking one's samayas has no merit in itself aside from the fact that such infractions can easily be purified. A broken samaya can be cleared up by confession, by remorsefully admitting one's fault. This is not the case in the lower vehicles. For example, when the vows of Individual Liberation, the Hinayana precepts for ordained and lay persons, are damaged, they are irretrievably lost. Like dropping a clay pot, it's irrevocably broken. Once a monk breaks one of the major vows, all two hundred and fifty-three precepts are broken and lost forever. These major vows cannot be mended again. But the samayas of Vajrayana are like a dent made in a jar of gold or silver: it's dropped, there is a dent, but the dent can be hammered out again and the jar will be fine.

There are four stages of severity: infraction, breach, violation, and complete break. Anything other than complete break is nothing more than a dent in a silver jar which can be repaired. One can mend damaged samayas by applying the four remedial powers, involving the chanting of the Hundred Syllable mantra, the quintessence of the mind of all the buddhas. Doing so will certainly repair any broken samaya. But the confession has to take place within three years; once three years have passed without a confession, the samaya is irrevocably broken and cannot be mended.

There are four powers of remedy to purify damaged samayas. The first is the power of support. At best it means to bring to mind the vivid presence of all the one hundred peaceful and wrathful deities. But, since all the hundred families are embodied in the single buddha, Vajrasattva, it is permissible to simply visualize Vajrasattva above the crown of one's head. To visualize either of these is called the power of the support.

Next is the power of the applied antidote which is like taking soap and water and washing our hands. The applied remedy is the practice of imagining the white syllable HUNG surrounded by the one hundred syllables in the heart center of Vajrasattva. From the mantra encircling the HUNG in the heart center, light radiates into all directions, making offerings to the buddhas and bodhisattvas. It also shines out to all sentient beings, purifying their veils and misdeeds. When this light is gathered back the nectar starts to drip down from Vajrasattva's heart center. The nectar comes out through his big toe and enters through the crown of one's head. This elixir of wisdom slowly purifies all of one's negative actions, veils, sicknesses, and evil influences. These leave the body through the lower openings. One should imagine the earth cracks open below to a depth of nine stories, where the Lord of Death and all his henchmen are standing waiting with open mouths. They greatly appreciate all the soot, pus and poisonous insects coming down, entering their gaping mouths and satisfying them, after which they too generate bodhichitta. Following that all one's karmic debts are cleared. To do the recitation, to imagine the negativity pouring down, and to be purified by the nectar is the second of the four powers called the power of the applied antidote.

The third, which is also really important, is the power of remorse. To go through the steps of the Vajrasattva practice without sincere remorse does not really purify our past negative actions. Honestly, a training in pretense is not effective. We must truly have deep regret for the misdeeds we can remember, as well as feel remorse for what we cannot remember. We have had plenty of past lives and the tendencies or karmic imprints of all our actions are still embedded in the all-ground consciousness right now. The Buddha has said that if we were to take the whole world and grind it into small pellets the size of a juniper berry, we could count those pellets, but we could not count how many lifetimes we have had. This example is used for developing bodhichitta, to illustrate how many mothers we have had in past lives. Just as we have had innumerable mothers, we have had countless lives, and all the negative actions we performed in those lives are latently present as habitual tendencies. Vajrasattva practice can purify all these latent tendencies for negative actions, but only if we have true remorse.

The most severe types of negative actions are known as the five actions with immediate results, meaning that the person who has committed any one of them goes straight to hell after death, without even passing through a bardo state. These five actions are to kill an arhat, one's father, or one's mother; to cause blood to flow from a buddha's body with evil intent; and to create a schism in the noble Sangha. But even the karma of such evil acts can be purified by calling upon the peaceful and wrathful deities or Buddha Vajrasattva in a gathering of one hundred practitioners of Vajrayana. One strips off all one's clothes and with a loud voice proclaims the misdeed to everyone present and to all the buddhas and bodhisattvas, saying, "In this whole world there is no one as evil as me. I have done such and such. May all the buddhas have pity on me! All you yogis and yoginis please help me by chanting the Hundred Syllable mantra!" Then one chants the Hundred Syllable mantra one hundred times while doing full prostrations, naked. Even the most severe negative action is purified by doing this. But, it is crucial to feel remorse.

The last of the four powers is the power of resolve, meaning to decide definitively that even at the cost of one's life one will not engage in a certain negative action again.

When one has developed these four powers, just a single session of chanting the Hundred Syllable mantra one hundred times can totally purify one's negative karma, although it may be as huge as Mount Sumeru. The practice of these four powers is as powerful as a match thrown onto a heap of dried grass the size of a mountain. Just put one match to it and the whole mountain burns down.

I have really been thinking about this, and the more I reflect on the practices of Vajrayana, of deity, mantra and samadhi, the more amazed I am. Really, these practices are incredible in purifying the latent tendencies in our minds which we have accumulated from countless lifetimes. It's only because these practices are so profound that all our misdeeds can totally be cleared away. Negative karma has no beneficial qualities, except that it can be cleared away in this manner. Were the effect of Vajrayana practice not so truly incredible, complete enlightenment would be impossible to achieve within a single lifetime. Of course, when the practices are profound the maras or demons get powerful too. Therefore it's important to have powerful practices and to really have trust. To practice Vajrayana teachings with mistrust, not believing that they are effective, doesn't help us much. In fact, such thinking is known as wrong view, and there is no worse misdeed than harboring wrong views. It's very important to trust that the Vajrayana practices are most wonderful.

In the Sutra system, one gathers the accumulations and purifies veils, slowly proceeding towards buddhahood, which is achieved after three incalculable eons. Incalculable is a name for the enormous number expressed by ten followed by fifty-two zeros, and refers to not just days, but eons. That is an incredibly long time. Through Vajrayana it is possible to attain complete enlightenment within this very body and lifetime. Think of that huge difference. Vajrayana training is not just attempting to be generous, disciplined, patient, diligent, concentrated and intelligent; to attain enlightenment through this alone would take three incalculable eons. Vajrayana practice is extremely deep. It is described as having many methods and few hardships, and is meant for people of sharp faculties. Those are the special qualities of Secret Mantra. If Vajrayana wasn't so ingenious, enlightenment in one lifetime wouldn't be possible. Vajrayana is extremely skilled in the methods for purifying obscurations and gathering the accumulations. Just think of the one deity, Vajrasattva, and one mantra, the Hundred Syllables—it's amazing.

Some people pretend to themselves that they don't have any negative karma and they are not creating any new negative karma either. They say, "I don't kill anybody. I don't lie. I commit no evil deeds!" But once we investigate the deluded state of mind, we understand that all evil deeds are done by the mind, and that this deluded state of mind is constantly busy making new negative karma. Unless we are in the state of rigpa, in which the three poisons are purified, any normal mind is continually engaging in one of the three mind poisons and is therefore constantly creating negative karma. There is no point in denying that. These subtle evil deeds—the feelings of attraction, dislike, and indifference—are like water moving under a covering of straw: the top of the straw is dry but the bottom is wet. How can we pretend to ourselves that we don't create negative karma?

There are two ways to purify one's obscurations; conventional and ultimate. The conventional way is to engage in the practices of visualizing, chanting, engendering remorse, and making resolutions. The ultimate practice is to purify the deluded state of mind by means of the threefold purity, by simply resting in rigpa, in nondual awareness. At that moment, what ties the whole of samsara together falls apart. The present misdeed is absent and the future one has not been created. In such a pure state of awareness all evil deeds and veils are purified. All negative karma is instantly purified, just as the darkness of ten thousand years is utterly cleared away the moment the light is switched on.

In the same way, that which connects one's mind with all the negative karma or imprints from the past is conceptual thinking. The moment conceptual thinking is absent there is nothing to tie samsara together; it is cut, just like a rope that has been cut cannot bind. Look into what samsara is based on, and see it is the moment-to-moment delusion. This string of deluded moments is known as the continuous instant of delusion, and is the basis of samsara. Among the five aggregates, it is called formation. The only thing that can really cut samsara is the moment of rigpa. Rigpa totally makes samsara fall apart.

The more I reflect on the Dharma, the more awe-struck I am. The Dharma teachings are amazing! It's like a true legacy that we can receive. The ordinary kind of legacy we receive when a businessman passes away helps us make money to take care of our body, right? Those are the instructions for continuing samsara. But what the Buddha has left and handed down to us are the instructions on how to empty samsara. That is something really incredible!

THE THREE
EXCELLENCES

Never forget the excellent preparation of bodhi-chitta, the excellent main part free from concepts and the excellent conclusion of dedicating the merit.

Tulku Urgyen Rinpoche

Grant your blessings that we may train in impartial love and
   compassion
And directly realize the ultimate co-emergent wisdom
As all the Buddhas and their sons and daughters have done.

By this virtue may all beings perfect the accumulations of merit and
   wisdom
And may they attain the sacred two kayas resulting from that merit
   and wisdom.

Buddhism traces its origins back to India, which is where it first appeared and where Buddha Shakyamuni attained complete enlightenment. Later the Dharma spread to other countries, including Nepal, and after that, to Tibet. Originally in India there were not many schools. Basically there were the two traditions of Sutra and Tantra, known as the vast and the profound teachings, and the four major schools of philosophy: Vaibhashika, Sautrantika, Mind Only and Middle Way.

However, when the teachings spread to Tibet, new lineages were named according to the varying periods of transmission. The first was the Old School, known as Nyingma. The subsequent seven lineages were called the New Schools. Altogether these different schools of teachings are known as the Eight Chariots of the Practice Lineage. They are Nyingma, Kadam, Sakya, and Karma Kagyü, then Shangpa Kagyü, Shijey and Chö, Jordruk, and Nyendrub. Today these are all included within the four schools of Tibetan Buddhism renowned as Nyingma, Kagyü, Gelug and Sakya.

All these schools are the flawless teachings of the enlightened ones and all practice the three excellences. When we practice the excellent preparation of bodhichitta, including both the relative and ultimate state of awakened mind; when we practice the main part of development stage and completion stage, free from concepts; and when we conclude with dedicating the merit and making aspirations for the welfare of others; we are combining all the teachings of Sutra and Tantra. These three excellences are thus extremely important. Any practice we do while possessing the three excellences is always correct, while any practice we do while lacking them is never really perfect.

We should always remember to embrace our practice with these three excellences, no matter how tiny or insignificant a deed may be. Even when we offer a single flower or just one stick of incense, or do one circumambulation around a sacred object, it is very important to first engender the proper motivation. We should think "I will do this to purify my obscurations and gather the accumulations in order to benefit all sentient beings." After completion, we should dedicate the merit for the welfare of everyone. In this way the virtue is multiplied immensely, so that the effect is one million times greater than simply doing a virtuous action without much thought about it.

The preparation is the proper motivation, created by invoking the vast attitude of Mahayana and the profound attitude of Vajrayana. The vast attitude of the bodhisattva or the Mahayana teachings is compassion. We consider all our parent sentient beings who are at present drowning in the immense ocean of samsaric existence, and make the aspiration that "I alone will rescue all these sentient beings and establish them in the precious state of complete enlightenment."

The profound attitude of Vajrayana is pure perception or sacred outlook, viewing all things as pure. The practice of Vajrayana entails imagining that the world is a buddhafield, our dwelling place is a celestial palace, all male and female beings are dakas and dakinis, all sounds are mantra, and that the thoughts and emotions of all sentient beings are the continuity of immense innate wakefulness. In this way, sights, sounds, and thoughts are perceived as the exalted mandala of deity, mantra, and wisdom. This is called training in seeing things as they really are, not superimposing something artificial.

The reason for the vast attitude of the bodhisattvas, their compassion, is that the Mahayana teachings are aimed at benefiting sentient beings in a number as infinite as space. Of all the six classes of beings, there is not a single one who has not been our own mother. But these beings do not know how to achieve happiness and instead continue sowing the seeds for samsaric existence. If we sincerely contemplate this, we cannot help but feel pity and compassion.

We usually feel love and affection for our father and mother in this life. Not only human beings experience this: there is also love between animal mothers and their young. If we understand that all beings have been our parents, there is no way for us as humans not to feel love for them. If we think about this, to whom do we owe the favor of having this human body we now possess? It is born from our parents and that is an immense kindness. Because of being alive we are able to practice the Dharma. Moreover, not only did our parents give us life, they raised us with loving care as well. If an infant is abandoned at birth it will not survive more than one or two days. But our parents, especially our mother, brought us up with tremendous kindness, undergoing great hardship. Shouldn't we feel gratitude?

Many people come to me and say, "I don't know how to feel compassion, how to cultivate it." Think like this: imagine that your mother is dragged before you by a sadistic murderer. He cuts off her ears, pulls out her tongue, gouges out her eyes, chops off her arms and legs and proceeds to cut up her body into small pieces. How would you feel towards your mother? It would be impossible not to feel pity and compassion for her. Thinking in this way about your mother, extend that feeling to all other sentient beings, because in actuality they too have been your mother. It's only a difference in time, nothing else. Is there any way we can avoid feeling compassion for all beings if we think like that?

The Buddha said that we have had many past lives, we have been born into innumerable physical bodies. If the bones from all our bodies in past lives were heaped together in a single pile, it would be taller than Mount Sumeru, the world mountain. In all these lives we have had parents; all sentient beings without a single exception whatsoever have been our own parents at some time. We should think of how to benefit them, how to return their kindness—not just to the parents of this life, but to all sentient beings without any prejudice or bias. This kind of attitude, not differentiating between sentient beings, is known as immeasurable impartiality, and is one of the four immeasurables. The idea of impartiality is viewing everyone as the same, not thinking that some people are my friends and others my enemies.

Now we cannot pretend to ourselves that we don't know how to generate compassion. But the vast attitude of a bodhisattva is not just compassion; it is the aspiration and the will to benefit and establish all beings without exception in the state of unsurpassable and supreme enlightenment.

Next, the excellent main part free from concepts refers mainly to the completion stage, but both development and completion are included within this context. First, development stage: the word "develop" means to create mentally, to visualize or imagine. The completion stage is the ultimate nature itself, free from any concepts. Holding concepts is the development stage; freedom from concepts is the completion stage.

In the development stage, imagine the outer world to be a buddha field. This is not regarding the world to be something that it is not, since everything is made out of the five elements, and the pure nature of the five elements is, since the very beginning, the five consorts of the five buddhas. In this respect, non-Buddhists of the ancient traditions as well as the Buddhists, possessed some pure perception of the world. The non-Buddhists did not regard the five elements to be ordinary or profane, but the nature of the various gods of earth, water, fire, and so forth. Vajrayana Buddhists regard the five elements in their pure nature as being the five female buddhas.

Furthermore, all beings without exception are comprised of the five elements and the five aggregates. In their impure aspect the five aggregates are physical forms, sensations, conceptions, formations, and cognitions. But in their pure aspect they are the five male buddhas. That is the reason for the statement 'all sentient beings are male and female deities.' The basis of speech is prana or wind, and the basis of wind is the wisdom wind which forms the dharanis, vidya-mantras, and guhya-mantras of all the enlightened ones. Also, the essence of all the thoughts and emotions of any sentient being is by nature primordial wakefulness, the mind of all the victorious ones. By training in pure perception in this way, we are not pretending that something is what it is not; we are simply acknowledging things for what they actually are, just like acknowledging that gold is gold.

In actuality, all sights, sounds, and thoughts are deities, mantra, and wisdom. Wisdom means the samadhi or the realized state of mind of the victorious ones. First of all we need to get the idea: this is known as regarding things to be what they are. In addition to the intellectual idea, we need the experience. Experience in this context means to recognize that the nature of consciousness is wisdom and that the essence of thought is nonconceptual wakefulness, and to leave the mind in its natural, fresh state. This is the excellent main part free from concepts.

To regard our body as the vajra body, our voice as vajra speech, and our mind as vajra mind, is known as development stage. In short, within the buddha nature resides the body, speech and mind of the victorious ones. The most important point is the ultimate development and completion stages, recognition of the buddha nature itself. Both development stage and completion stage are aspects of the buddha nature. It is said development stage is skillful means, while completion stage is discriminating knowledge, prajna. We should not separate the stages of development and completion, the means and knowledge aspects of Vajrayana.

The mandala of deities, mantra, and wisdom means that all appearances have the nature of deities, all sounds are the nature of mantra, and all thoughts are the nature of enlightened mind. This is the profound attitude of Secret Mantra, that sights are deities, sounds are mantra, thoughts are wisdom. This falls under what I mentioned before concerning Gampopa's third teaching, "Grant your blessings that the path may clarify confusion!" It encompasses the development stage. Completion stage falls under Gampopa's fourth teaching, "Grant your blessings that confusion may dawn as wisdom!" In this context, the views of Mahamudra, Dzogchen, and Madhyamika are all just different names for our buddha nature. These three are not different, and their meeting point is the buddha nature.

The excellent conclusion of dedication has two parts: dedicating the merit and making aspirations. In order to dedicate we need to have performed a positive deed, for instance, repeating even just once the mantra OM MANI PADME HUNG HRIH. "Preceded by a virtuous deed" means that we have created something virtuous so that its effect can be dedicated to the welfare of all beings. Next, the aspiration is to think "May all deeds and intentions of the buddhas and bodhisattvas of all directions and times be fulfilled!"

Once something positive, even though conceptual, is created, if we forget to dedicate the merit or make aspirations, getting angry will destroy the virtue. We can create two kinds of virtue: conditioned and unconditioned. Conditioned virtue means something we think or intend conceptually. Anger is also conditioned, and conditioned anger can destroy conditioned virtue. Unconditioned virtue, the practice of the view, is like pure space. It is beyond change and cannot be destroyed. Conditioned virtue is like a cloud which can be blown away by the wind; but unconditioned virtue is like the sky itself, which cannot be blown away by wind. But once we dedicate the merit and make aspirations nothing can destroy the effect of our virtuous practice. It is finished, done with. The reason why we should never forget to dedicate the merit is because we are ordinary people and we do get angry. It is possible. That anger just wastes our conceptual merit.

On the other hand, if we can seal the conditioned virtue with unconditioned virtue, with what is known as threefold purity—resting in the state of self-existing awareness without holding any concept of subject, object, and action—this threefold purity will ensure that the conditioned virtue is never destroyed.

When we dedicate the merit, usually we think there is the virtuous action that I did, there is the object to whom I will dedicate it, all sentient beings, and then there is me doing it. That setup is conditioned, conceptual. Threefold means endowed with the three concepts. When free from these three concepts, what is left? There is only self-existing awareness, threefold purity. Free from the notions of subject, object, and act of dedication, we automatically arrive in the original pure state which is as inexhaustible as an ocean of virtue. In the sutras this is called sealing the virtuous deed with emptiness. In, the Sanskrit word for emptiness—*shunyata*—*shunya* means being free from even an atom of material substance, while the *ta* signifies that self-existing cognizance is present.

OBSTACLES

With your kindness, bestow your blessings upon me.
With your affection, guide myself and others on the path.
With your realization, grant me the siddhis.
With your powers, dispel the obstacles of myself and others.
Clear the outer obstacles externally.
Clear the inner obstacles internally.
Clear the secret obstacles into space.
Respectfully I bow down and take refuge in you.
OM AH HUNG VAJRA GURU PADMA SIDDHI HUNG

Clearing the Obstacles on the Path,
a terma of Chokgyur Lingpa

Generally speaking, there are three types of obstacles: the outer obstacles of the four elements, the inner obstacles of the channels, winds and essences, and the secret obstacles of dualistic fixation.

To dispel outer obstacles there are the three aspects of approach, accomplishment, and the activities, which are connected to the sadhanas of guru, yidam, and dakini. One of the most renowned methods is the *Barchey Künsel* cycle of teachings, which is primarily concerned with dispelling obstacles. The *Barchey Lamsel* prayer found within this cycle of teachings says, "Clear the outer obstacles externally. Clear the inner obstacles internally. Clear the secret obstacles into space." To clear away the inner obstacles of imbalances in the channels, winds and essences, tummo practice is the most eminent. To overcome the obstacles of clinging to subject and object, there is no better remedy than simply maintaining the correct view.

The outer obstacles of the four elements are defined as earth, water, fire and wind. For example, we can understand the obstacle of earth to be an earthquake, the obstacle of water to be flooding, the obstacle of fire our house catching fire and the obstacle of wind to be a hurricane. These types of destruction do occur and they can be averted by certain sadhanas to pacify the four outer elements.

The inner obstacles involve the channels, winds, and essences of our physical body. We should also understand that the four major elements are contained within the body. Flesh and bones are the earth element, blood is the water element, the heat of the body is the fire element, and the breath is the wind element. Inner obstacles occur when the balance between the channels, winds, and essences is disturbed. The circulation is somehow blocked, giving rise to all different kinds of sickness. These imbalances, the inner obstacles, can be cleared up through what the New Schools call the six doctrines of Naropa. The Nyingma system has the same six teachings. The main one, known as the life pillar, is tummo practice, which belongs to the Anu Yoga level of teaching. The inner obstacles can be pacified by becoming adept in these practices of channels, winds and essences.

Secret obstacles are grasping at objects outwardly and fixating on the perceiver inwardly, and are therefore called grasping and fixation. The *Barchey Lamsel* prayer says, "Clear the outer obstacles externally. Clear the inner obstacles internally. Clear the secret obstacles into space." This means that in the moment of recognizing nondual awareness, grasping and fixation both dissolve into the innate space of dharmadhatu. When obstacles are cleared away, attainment occurs by itself, spontaneously. Obstacles are what prevent the two kinds of accomplishment, common and supreme.

As an example, imagine ancient traders sailing the ocean to the end of the world, to an island of jewels.

They gather up the jewels and return to enjoy great profit; that's gaining accomplishment without obstacles. But if the traders had problems on the way—if a hurricane or ocean monsters wrecked the ship and they drowned—they would lose their lives, instead of bringing back valuable jewels. That's a mundane example for being overcome by obstacles.

We should utilize this life completely to achieve the two kinds of accomplishments, especially the supreme accomplishment of complete enlightenment. The only things that truly prevent enlightenment are the secret obstacles of grasping and fixation. Certainly outer obstacles of the four elements can be problematic. Earthquakes, floods, fires, and hurricanes do take people's lives, as do the inner obstacles of sicknesses. But it is most essential to clear away the secret obstacles. Only the secret obstacles can really prevent buddhahood. As long as we haven't reached enlightenment we are always keeping company with these obstacles.

Another way of looking at obstacles is known as the four maras or the four demons. The first of these is the demon of the Lord of Death, which cuts our life short. Second is the demon of the physical aggregates, which prevents the attainment of the rainbow body. Third is the demon of the disturbing emotions, the three poisons which prevent liberation from samsara. Finally there is the demon of the son of the gods, which is distraction in the meditation state and the tendency to postpone practice, thinking, "Well, today I didn't get around to practicing but tomorrow I will for sure, and if I can't tomorrow, I will certainly do it the day after!" Or, "This year I couldn't really concentrate on practice, but next year I will definitely do an intensive retreat." Procrastination is the mara of the son of the gods, which creates obstacles for samadhi.

Where do these four maras live? Where is their home? It is said that the mara of the disturbing emotions dwells in the red and white elements within the body. The mara of the physical aggregates dwells in the flesh, bones, and skin. The mara of the Lord of Death dwells in the life channel, while the mara of the son of the gods dwells in our mind. The demon of the kleshas constantly creates new disturbing emotions. Finally, the demon of the son of the gods constantly distracts our concentration in meditation practice. It is like a small voice that says, "You can always practice tomorrow, or the day after!" In short, the demons that make obstacles are not outside ourselves; they are within.

One day, we never know when, the demon of the Lord of Death will cut our life force and we will die. The demon of the physical aggregates prevents our departure from this world without leaving a corpse behind. Everybody who has not achieved the realization of the rainbow body dies with a corpse. But great accomplished practitioners either depart in a transformed body to the celestial realms, or attain the rainbow body, in which case the physical body simply vanishes.

Each of these four maras has an army of twenty thousand small demons, so all together there are eighty thousand types of obstructers. They are like a huge force waiting to attack us, armed with their weapons, the 80,000 kinds of disturbing emotions. The 80,000 obstructers carry the four hundred and four sicknesses: the four primary sicknesses caused by the various combinations of wind, gall, phlegm, and their combination. Each of these has a hundred subsidiary aspects, making 404 altogether. Figuratively speaking, one is surrounded by a huge army of 80,000 obstructing demons armed with the lethal weapons of disease. In the center of this huge horde of pitiless demons and obstacles is one's life force trying to maintain itself, trying to subsist.

The leader of this great army of 80,000 demons is the king of demons, who is known as Garab Wangchuk, the "Lord of Pleasure." He stays in one of the divine abodes in the Realm of Form. Looking down from here, he can see all the realms below as clearly as looking at the palm of his hand. From below however, we can't see the realms above when we look up. Garab Wangchuk is always on watch, and he cannot bear it if he sees anyone about to slip away into liberation or enlightenment. To help him, he has five queens, named for the five poisons: one is known as Attachment, one is Pride, one is Anger, one is Jealousy and one is called Stupidity. Day and night, they look down into this world with ill will, keeping constant guard, like an elaborate spy system. They look for anyone doing Dharma practice and try to close the door to liberation.

As soon as they see that somebody, particularly a stable person, is trying to practice, making the resolution, "Now I will engage in learning, reflection and meditation! I will practice the Dharma to attain liberation and enlightenment!", they get very upset and say, "We can't allow that to happen!" The five queens take up their special weapons, the bows and arrows of the five poisons. Letting loose an arrow, they shoot it right into the practitioner's heart, using either attachment, anger or stupidity, depending on which poison he or she is most prone to. For example, if someone is most vulnerable to stupidity, they shoot the arrow of ignorance; likewise with desire, anger, pride or jealousy. The queens are constantly shooting down arrows onto people trying to attain liberation. They especially target those who are trying to accomplish the Dharma, who are susceptible to obstacles, and who they can harm. The main perpetrator, of course, is Garab Wangchuk, closely followed by his retinue of queens, armed with the five poisons, and the four demons. In addition, Garab Wangchuk has the eighty thousand different kinds of obstacle makers to help him. It's like an evil force trying to undermine practitioners. Their special weapon is the fourth of the maras, the demon of the son of the gods, which is not only the tendency to postpone meditation but also the tendency to feel either dull, distracted or agitated when practicing, as well as to feel doubt and make superfluous plans during the meditation sessions.

Practitioners who are susceptible or vulnerable to obstacles are most affected. As Lodrö Thaye said, "When I engage in Dharma practice I fall under the power of dullness and drowsiness. When I engage in nondharmic activities I am clear and bright with sharp faculties." This is because of the help we get from Garab Wangchuk. For example, if someone has the chance to stay up and gamble for high stakes, he can be awake the whole night and doesn't feel sleepy at all. But if he sits down and chants OM MANI PADME HUNG, he falls asleep after five minutes. That's called falling under the power of mara. There's another saying, "The more profound the Dharma practice, the more crafty the demons." When one tries to practice the Dharma obstacles immediately arise.

Often it happens that one meets obstacles when practicing the Dharma—one falls sick, outer circumstances don't really work out, the aims one pursues are unsuccessful. Something always seems to go wrong, one experiences unhappiness and so forth. But if one looks around, it seems that people who cheat others, who are liars and pretenders, are really successful. Take the example of Mao Tse Tung, who was able to control the whole of China. In many other countries as well there are big demons in human form, who possess incredible good fortune, long life, excellent health, and tremendous wealth. Seeing this, many people lose heart and say, "Maybe it's better not to practice Dharma. Look at what happens! Practitioners are poor, they wear uninteresting clothes, they don't eat well, they barely survive; whereas people who cheat others are rich and lucky, and have long life and good health. Maybe it's better not to practice the Dharma. Maybe it's better to be a crook." Believe it or not, many people think it's better not to practice the Dharma, because obviously it doesn't really make us successful in this life. But people who think in that way don't understand what is really happening. When somebody cheats and grabs power and is really demonic, his undeniable success is simply because all his merit is being spent in this very lifetime. These kind of people quickly finish all the good merit they had from past lives. Likewise, while it might appear that practitioners are unfortunate and unlucky, it is only because all their past bad karma is coming to an end in this very life. In the future they will just go up to higher and higher states.

That's one way to understand this point. Another way is that all the things we think define success in this world—money, good health and so forth—are all left behind when this life is over. The Dharma practitioner staying with just a minimum of requirements in the mountains or a cave without being socially successful is spending his life on something that will help in all his future lives.

In short, not understanding the law of karma and looking at other people, one could have the thought that maybe it's better not to practice Dharma. Someone concerned only with the superficial value of things is unable to see that past merit is being rapidly exhausted by people who act like criminals, while practitioners are purifying their past negative karma. It is certainly true that practitioners have more obstacles than normal people, but one shouldn't think because of this that negative actions are more profitable than Dharma practice.

Two points of mind training are important to take to heart. One is that when we have positive conditions and good fortune, and everything seems to be working out, we should think, "This is thanks to the Three Jewels! This is happening not just because I am bright and wonderful, but due to the virtues of the Three Jewels." Likewise, when we are unsuccessful, disappointed, frustrated, or sick, or when things simply don't work out, we should think, "Now my negative karma from the past is being used up. How nice!" We shouldn't be like business people, whose faces become like the sky covered with dark clouds when they lose in trade. It is much better to have the attitude that whatever good is happening is not because I am special or I did something unique; it's more beneficial to think that it happens due to the kindness of the Three Jewels. Thinking in that way multiplies our merit. Conversely, when meeting with difficulties, instead of feeling overwhelmed and saying, "How terrible! I can't take this!", just say, "How nice! Now my negative karma is being used up and I am rid of that!", and then rejoice in the difficulties. Training your mind in this way will help increase the merit and ensure that all negative karma is brought to an end.

DHARMA PRACTICE
AND WORLDLY AIMS

We commit our life to Dharma practice,
We commit our Dharma practice to living in poverty.
We commit our poverty to dwelling in solitude,
We commit our solitude to last until death.

from the Oral Tradition of the Kadampas

Actually, spiritual practice and worldly aims are like two irreconcilable enemies that will never get along. Trying to house these two together is like having a friend and a foe under the same roof: no matter how one deals with it, it's not easy. The main reason the Buddha gave up his palace, his queen, and all his wealth was because Dharma practice and worldly aims are essentially incompatible. The Buddha demonstrated that one embraces spiritual training by leaving worldly concerns behind.

On the other hand, if one has already submerged oneself into the illusion of family life, one can't just leave that. One has to take responsibility for one's family. As the West lacks the tradition of renunciate life, it is admittedly difficult for Westerners to forsake everything—career, luxuries and social standing. In Tibet, certain individuals could give up everything and focus one hundred percent on practicing the Dharma, and somehow, they would still get by. Lay people would support practitioners and devotedly give donations and food to meditators living in seclusion in caves and quiet places. In this way, the benefactor created the link for attaining enlightenment at the same time as the practitioner.

I don't think it's like that in the West. It appears to me that foreigners simply wanting to practice the Dharma intensively are not necessarily supported by other people. So a renunciate life is difficult in the West. One has to take responsibility for one's personal livelihood: that's the Western way, so that's what has to be followed. Try to make the best of it so that you can carry on your mundane life and at the same time not give up the Dharma. If one gives up the Dharma, there certainly won't be any progress; definitely don't do that. If one gives up worldly life it's very, very difficult also. Try to do both at the same time.

People who in the earlier part of their life are work-oriented can focus more on Dharma practice in the latter part of their lives. That is supposed to be a sign of a good disciple. But if a Dharma practitioner starts out by renouncing everything and later becomes a businessman, that is the opposite: in fact, it's called "the bad son of a good father." Of course, everything is impermanent and we cannot really be sure of how much time we have. Still, one could plan, "As soon as I have relinquished my responsibilities and I am not completely in need of money, then I will focus as much as I can on Dharma practice." One can wish to be able to focus the latter part of one's life on Dharma practice.

But until you get to the point of being free from responsibilities, try to be diligent and practice as much as possible in your present situation. One doesn't work all twenty-four hours, there is still free time in a day. You might have to work in the daytime, but at night don't be too generous with the pleasures of sleep. Try to be a moderate sleeper, and also spend some time practicing in the early morning. Practice instead of just loafing. Since Western people work only seven or eight hours a day, of course there is time to practice.

Why did I say that mundane aims and religious life are mutually exclusive? The aims of a normal worldly person are to acquire food—good food—and of course the money to back it up. Worldly people also strive for expensive clothes, a pleasant situation, a good reputation, fame, and so forth, whereas a Dharma practitioner tries to diminish those needs. He or she looks for just enough money to get by, and wears clothes given by other people, cast-off, second-hand garments. Practitioners regard fame as an evil. A practitioner who dreams that he is famous should regard that as an obstacle of mara.

Think about it! Fame is just like the name tagged to a corpse. After one dies, one's reputation will not be of any help to the mind that travels on. The messengers of the Lord of Death in the bardo state will not respect someone just because he was famous.

The Dharma practitioner and the worldly person are oriented in completely opposite directions. The Kadampa teaching known as the Four Commitments says: "We commit our life to Dharma practice. We commit our Dharma practice to living in poverty. We commit our poverty to dwelling in solitude. We commit our solitude to last until death." Isn't that the opposite of normal worldly aims? A normal person wants to accomplish the things of this life, mundane attainments. He wants to become rich and stay in a nice mansion with many people around; forget about dying all alone in a remote place.

If, however, you already have a family then try to combine earning a living with spiritual practice; that's the best way. After a few years when there is less responsibility—assuming that there are enough years later, because we honestly don't know—go to some quiet mountain place and wave a final goodbye to the futile aims of worldly life.

The old masters of the past taught repeatedly that one should devote one's mind one hundred percent to Dharma practice and give up worldly life. They still teach this, but for disciples to follow this literally is very, very difficult. On the other hand, if one has a job, while one is working, again and again, recognize mind essence; then continue working. That will bring very good results. In Tibet the people who exclusively taught spiritual practice were called lamas. These days the only lama who teaches both worldly life and Dharma practice is me. A lama is only supposed to teach Dharma practice, not both. I'm just joking.

Try to practice in the correct way at least a small percentage, a fraction of the time, like an imitation of real practice. The essence of Dharma is to take this to heart: now we have some free will, there are choices we can make, we have some control over our lives, some kind of independent power. During this period of being alive in a human body, when we have such freedom, we can use it in a positive way. As soon as this life is over, when the breath stops, this body is just a heap of dead matter—it becomes a corpse. The moment the body is abandoned by your mind it is like a ruin, an abandoned house, and will never come back to life. When body and mind have separated there is no longer any freedom, no longer a choice to make. One has no independent power to control anything. Instead, one is under the power of one's karma, the unfailing law of cause and result. One is under the power of one's positive and negative karma.

In this life, we don't need to try to accomplish black karma; it occurs automatically. One needs to accomplish white karma, to prepare for the time when one will have no independent choice. One needs to work now on developing control. That is the main point. There is no greater profit in Dharma practice than that.

Most people think when they hear about profit that it's a matter of providing food to eat. But the profit of Dharma practice is not something one can see. As soon as the breath has stopped and there is no free will or control, the real profit at that time is to have developed free will. In order to develop this free will, one depends on one's current action, one's Dharma practice. That is what gives one free will. Now when we are independent we are able to practice the Dharma, and by doing so, we are able to gain control or free will. If we practice the view, meditation, and action right now, later, when the body and mind separate, we will be able to remember the Dharma.

About practicing in quietude or practicing in distraction: the traditional way is that first one practices in solitude. There are the three solitudes of body, speech and mind. Through these three one accomplishes the vajra body, vajra speech, and vajra mind. But the main idea of going to remote places where one is free from distraction is to apply the teachings and attain mastery over the body, speech and mind of the victorious ones.

If one is unable to practice in solitude for long periods, one can sometimes go to a quiet place for a short while. There is benefit from concentrating on practice even for a few days or a month. During one's daily life when one is distracted and continuously gets carried away, try to practice the recognition of mind nature as short moments, repeated many times. If it is a short moment that is the genuine moment of unadulterated recognition. 'Many times' means that unless it is repeated often, one will never become accustomed to it. Try to practice like that as much as possible. All the Kagyü and Nyingma lamas say that one should practice short moments repeated many times. They never said long sessions with few repetitions.

After the practitioner becomes stable to some extent in the recognition of the innate nature, the unadulterated awareness free from distraction, he goes to the marketplace to interact with other people. The practice then is to mingle awareness with the daily activities of eating, moving about, sitting, and sleeping. One tries to see whether one's stability is in any way influenced by external experiences. The best is if there is no effect, if nothing harms or benefits one's recognition.

When one has totally mingled the state of nondual awareness with the situations of daily life, it does not matter whether or not one stays in remote places. Whatever one does is an expression of awareness. Since one has attained stability in practice, everything arises within a wide-open view—this is known as "cutting through." It is said that "one's experience manifests as helpers and turns into symbols and books." For the practitioner accustomed to the view, there isn't a hair-tip of harm from social interaction.

We need to gain control over the liberated state of mind right now, before we die. An essential point in Dharma is to attain stability in recognizing our buddha nature now, while we have the ability and opportunity. When we die and the mind leaves the body, it is a completely different situation. The mind in the material body is said to be like a chained crow; it cannot fly off. But the moment the mind leaves the body and becomes a bardo consciousness, we no longer have any control over circumstances. For a normal person the bardo state is totally chaotic, just like a feather blowing in a hurricane.

That is why we have to practice right now. The real profit is to be fully prepared for the time when there is no free will. Right now we have some degree of control: we can do what we want, go where we please, lie in the sun, eat whatever we like. But sooner or later everyone dies. Nothing stops that, and at that time there is no more freedom to make choices. Therefore, decide right now which is better—the futile struggle to achieve temporary worldly aims, or the lasting benefit accomplished through practicing the Dharma.

If one is earnest, if one is clever, one will make the right choice between just getting through life as if that is an end in itself, and attaining stability in nondual awareness, in the original awakened state. When given these two choices by the lama, an intelligent person will know which to choose.

We don't really know when we are going to die. If we don't truly have trust in the Buddhist teachings or the teacher, it is not going to help that much to read this, because we won't pay much attention to it. Even if a clairvoyant told us, "This is your last day, you are going to die tomorrow!", we won't believe that; we'll just say, "How does he know anything! What is he talking about, I am young and healthy, I don't have any sickness!" If we don't believe, it won't help at all. But a smart person with trust will know which is better. He will reject wallowing in samsaric worldly life and being unprepared for the time of no control, and instead endeavor in the practices that will give him control at the time of death. A clever person will understand. The main point is to arrive at the point where one keenly feels, "I should practice Dharma, I should practice Dharma!"

Right now our body is like a guesthouse and the mind is like a traveler. For this lifetime we are staying in one guesthouse. There is some sense of grounding due to the mind being in a body, but there isn't any real stability. Once body and mind separate, we have no control over what happens or where we go. As soon as the body dies, the mind is completely unsupported. One is left ungrounded, and is carried away by the wind of karma. Quite frankly, we don't possess any real stability right now. It is quite easy to ascertain this: just see whether your mind can actually remain stable for even one day. Try to concentrate on one thing, for example, your country or a place in your country, continuously from morning to evening. Are you able to do so?

As a matter of fact our minds are totally unstable, and we have no real control over them. They flutter about from one thing to the next, quite scattered. If we experience this while we still have the support of a physical body, imagine how it will be without the physical body, when the mind is naked and bare. At that time the mind directly experiences the ripening of past karma without any shield of a physical body, which is incredibly overwhelming. Think about this.

When one is a bardo consciousness everything is totally uncertain—where one goes, who one is with, what one eats. Everything is totally unpredictable; one is like a feather blowing in a hurricane. Some people find comfort in thinking that death is just like a fire that was put out or water that dried up. But death isn't at all like that. According to the words of the fully enlightened Buddha and the many texts of the bodhisattvas, the mind doesn't die. When the body dies, the mind remains under the power of habitual patterns and karma. Thus, those who trust the Buddha and the tradition he inspired will believe in birth, death, and the cause and effect of karmic actions.

Once one has attained stability in self-existing wisdom one will know that all that appears and exists, the world and the beings, are just the magical display of deluded mind. One will also have confidence in all the qualities of the fully enlightened Buddha as described in the scriptures.

Try and check right now: does your mind have any stability or control? Does it remain in the body or can it freely go outside the body? If we really had any control, we could right now decide to simply drop and be finished forever with all disturbing emotions. But does that happen? Can we do that? Also, if we had control we could easily acquire all the great qualities of wisdom and compassion of the buddhas. We could merely say, "Let these qualities be present!", and instantly we would have them. Does that happen? It doesn't, does it?

Really think well about how it will be in the bardo without the support of a body. What it comes down to is the importance of right now recognizing and training in mind essence, because that is the only way to gain stability. Everything else is unfixed, unstable, and uncertain. Only buddha nature is permanent. The buddha nature is the only thing possessing stability. Buddha nature has the four qualities of transcendent purity, permanence, bliss, and identity. Nothing else possesses these qualities.

We should decide right now if we do or do not have control over our mind. When we die, we won't have any power to influence where we go or where we stay, what we can eat or what we can do. We won't have even one second of control. It's complete horror to be a bardo consciousness carried by the wind of karma. Think well about whether we have control. If we have control now, then certainly we'll be able to have control in the bardo. However, truthfully, right now does your mind, even for a short while, have the power to go or stay anywhere?

The only way to really acquire all the great qualities of enlightenment is to repeat many times the short moment of recognizing mind essence. There is no other method. One reason for short moments is that because there is no stability right now, the recognition of awareness doesn't last for more than a brief moment, whether we like it or not. By practicing many times, one gets used to it. It is not that one is doing something conceptual like meditating upon an object or keeping a thing in mind. We simply need to recognize naked awareness, to allow for a moment of the awakened state of mind. It is not like we have to create something.

As we become increasingly accustomed to the state of naked awareness, slowly and gradually we will eliminate its opposite, the bad habits of dualistic fixation, disturbing emotions and creating negative karma that we have been used to for so long. Otherwise, if we had stability right now we could simply decide, "I'll recognize mind essence!", and remain like that forever. If we really had stability we could just recognize that the essence of our minds is dharmakaya and then that's it. Unfortunately, this doesn't happen.

The method to gain control is pointed out when the lama introduces you to your own buddha nature. As one becomes used to recognizing awareness, discursive thinking diminishes. There is no other way to do this. We can't simply order ignorance away and command rigpa to come forth and stay. Examine that yourself: can you do so? That is what I mean by saying there is no real stability yet. A sentient being is someone who is completely carried away by distraction.

Here's an example for the mind let loose in the bardo state: take a wild horse, one totally untrained, which has never worn a bridle or had a bit in its mouth or a saddle on its back. Catch one of those, put on a saddle, bridle, and a lot of packing gear, then let it go. The horse will be totally terrified. It won't know what anything is, and will just gallop away until it drops because it doesn't have any self-control. We are like that; we don't have any control. Control is to be free of all defects and to possess all qualities, like the Buddha. At the present time the situation is not as bad as it could be because we are still in a physical body, like a bird that is tied or a horse that is tethered. But the moment we die we are totally ungrounded, like the wild horse just galloping off.

One way to describe this is that if somebody falls asleep they can dream. If they haven't fallen asleep, like the example of the fully enlightened Buddha, they do not dream. The buddhas are like somebody who never fell asleep and are therefore not dreaming, not in delusion, whereas sentient beings are like someone asleep. Just as all dreams take place within the sleeping state, likewise all that we know, see, and feel takes place within the framework of dualistic mind. The state of experience shared by all sentient beings is like dreaming while being asleep, the sleep of ignorance. What is the difference between awareness and dualistic mind? Awareness is like someone not sleeping, who is totally undeluded, primordially free. Dualistic mind is tied down by our experience and is completely carried away by delusion. Like the dream state, it is rooted in the unreal.

Right now it seems like we have to get rid of something and we have to attain something: we have to get rid of ignorance and the disturbing emotions, and we have to attain rigpa. That is quite true on a certain level, and the only way to do that is to practice. However, enlightenment is never attained as long as duality remains. As long as we have two things—as long as we have to get rid of one thing and attain another—duality remains. Everything must become oneness in the recognition of mind essence, then there is no duality.

Right now, the mind is totally unstable. Even if everybody in the Kathmandu Valley tried to help your mind stay without moving, it would not. It is only through the practice of mind essence that true stability is attained. If you really think about this, you will understand that such a teaching is truly precious, something very special. First we should get the idea, then think about it, experience it, and finally realize it. That is what the Buddha said. There isn't any other method.

BARDO

When my time has come and impermanence and death have
    caught up with me,
When the breath ceases, and the body and mind go their separate
    ways,
May I not experience delusion, attachment, and clinging,
But remain in the natural state of dharmakaya.

Longchenpa

The general teachings outline six bardos. Two of these, the bardo of meditation and the bardo of dreams, occur within the bardo of this life, which is defined as the period following birth until the onset of death. The actual process of passing away is known as the bardo of dying. The bardo of dharmata occurs immediately after death, with the cessation of the outer and inner breath. Finally, the consciousness seeking a new rebirth is the bardo of becoming.

In essence, the bardos of dying, dharmata and becoming correspond to the three kayas. They do so in the sense that when you properly apply the instructions, you can attain dharmakaya at the moment of death. If not, you have the opportunity to attain the sambhogakaya level in the bardo of dharmata, or at least to attain the level of a nirmanakaya in the bardo of becoming.

The bardo of dying is when one is just about to pass away, but has not yet completely expired. Utilizing the key points of the oral instructions at that time, one can attain the dharmakaya level of realization. But if one is unable to do so, the peaceful and wrathful deities will manifest in one's experience during the bardo of dharmata. These deities are our own innate divinities appearing to ourselves, not gods coming from somewhere else to bless or haunt us. Some people deny the existence of the peaceful and wrathful deities, saying that these forms are just imaginary creations. On the contrary, they are not a product of our imagination; neither are they created through years of meditation. They are not something that we construct, even as a projection. The peaceful and wrathful buddhas are primordial: as manifestations of the primordial pure essence, they are by nature spontaneously present.

Right now we are in the bardo of this life, the bardo of conditioned entities or *dharmas* (not to be confused with *dharmata*, which means the unconditioned nature). What we experience at present seems very solid and real. Through our senses we perceive outer objects, other people, and the world. Yet it's not our senses that perceive; it is our mind. The mind uses the senses to experience the world. But the bardo of dharmata is perceived directly through the faculty of mind. The peaceful and wrathful deities and all the sounds, colors, and lights experienced at that time are empty apparitions, appearances lacking any real nature. Although they are extremely overwhelming and even terrifying, they are insubstantial, just like rainbows.

In our present situation, these deities form the buddha mandala of our body. Actually, our body is a palace of deities. The buddha nature is the basic deity, and our body is its palace. At the time of death our innate deities emerge, and we can be deluded by our own self-display, just as is said in a proverb, "The deceased is frightened by his innate deities, like the wild donkey is frightened by mountain grass moving in the wind." In Tibet the mountain grass sometimes moves in a way that could make a donkey think there was some animal chasing him, when in reality it was just empty movement in the grass. The apparitions of the peaceful and wrathful deities that are inherently present in our body will terrify the untrained practitioner, but these apparitions are actually our own manifestations.

Our familiarity with the practice of rigpa right now ensures that when we enter the bardo of dharmata it will be like meeting an old friend, someone we know very well. We will be able to recognize all the apparitions, sounds, colors, and lights as our natural display, the manifestation of our own buddha nature. Doing so, we can be liberated into the level of sambhogakaya.

If we are unable to recognize the basic state of awareness during the bardo of dharmata, the bardo of becoming unfolds. To those who have kept their samayas pure, six recollections appear during the bardo of becoming: the recollections of the yidam, the path, the place of rebirth, the meditative state, the oral instructions of the teacher, and the view. If we remember the practice at this point, we will take rebirth in a nirmanakaya buddhafield. Thus, the individual of the lowest degree of practice is liberated into nirmanakaya in the bardo of becoming.

The most important thing is how we apply the teachings of the six bardos to our own practice. Most vital is the present instant of recognizing rigpa, especially at the time of the four experiences during the bardo of dying. For normal people there are only three experiences, but for practitioners there are four: appearance, increase, attainment, and the ground luminosity of full attainment.

The first of these four, appearance, is known as the experience of whiteness, in which the white element obtained from our father descends from the crown of the head down towards the heart center. This is accompanied by the dissolution of the thirty-three types of aggressive thought states. The next experience is increase or the experience of redness, which takes place when the red element obtained from our mother ascends from below the navel up to the heart center. It is accompanied by the dissolution of the forty types of thought states linked to desire.

The meeting of the red and white elements is known as attainment or the experience of blackness, and is accompanied by the dissolution of the seven thought states of stupidity. All the eighty innate thought states cease when the red and white elements meet at the heart center. Ordinary people who have not recognized rigpa have no experience or familiarity with a state that is awake, yet free from conceptual thought. They experience a blackout at this moment, becoming blank and unconscious. This oblivious state lasts for three and a half days, after which the mind wakes up and suddenly finds itself in the bardo of dharmata.

For the practitioner familiar with the fourth state, the ground luminosity of full attainment, enlightenment can take place very easily at the moment of death. For the trained practitioner, the meeting of the red and white elements unveils an experience that is neither oblivious nor conceptual, and which in essence is the same as the nondualistic awareness we can recognize right now. Conceptual thinking is not present during the recognition of rigpa, yet there is no oblivion either. Attaining familiarity and stability in awareness while we are alive will ensure that we do not fall unconscious when the fourth moment, the ground luminosity of full attainment, unfolds. At the concluding moment of the three experiences, the sequence of recognition, stability, and liberation occurs as quickly as flapping the sleeve of a Tibetan robe three times. It takes no longer than that to attain enlightenment. As is said in *Chanting the Names of Manjushri*, "One moment makes all the difference; in one moment, complete enlightenment."

The crucial point in the context of the two elements converging in the heart center is the experience of the fourth moment, the ground luminosity of rigpa. The experience of the white and red element joining together is the same experience that grabbed the consciousness out of the bardo and into this life to begin with. It occurred when we were conceived into the womb, at the time when the mother's and father's red and white element joined together. In that moment of bliss-emptiness the consciousness fainted and was then conceived. Therefore it's extremely important to not fall oblivious but to remain awake and detached.

The dissolution of the elements occurs before the real death takes place. There are gross, subtle, and very subtle dissolution stages. The gross ones involving the dissolution of the five elements are felt by everybody and occur before the breathing stops. First the earth element starts to disintegrate, and one feels really heavy. That's when people say, "Please lift me up! I feel like I'm sinking! Raise me up!" When the water element dissolves one feels very cold and says "Please warm me up. It's too cold in here!" When the fire element dissolves one feels very thirsty and wants water; one's lips are drying up. When the wind element dissolves one feels as if one is drifting away at the brink of an abyss, not anchored anywhere. After the four elements have dissolved, consciousness dissolves into space, and everything grows vast and completely ungrounded. At this point the outer breath has stopped but the inner breathing is still circulating.

The subtle dissolution stage is made up of the three experiences of appearance, increase, and attainment. These occur while the outer breath has stopped but the inner breath, the inner circulation of energy-currents, has not yet ceased. For most people they don't take very long—just one, two, three. The redness experience is like the red light of the setting sun spreading throughout one's vision. The whiteness is like moonlight, and the blackness is like everything going completely dark. At the moment the white and red elements converge at the heart center, one experiences the unity of bliss and emptiness and either falls unconscious, or, if one is a practitioner who has familiarity with the state of rigpa, one experiences the ground luminosity of full attainment, the basic state of primordial purity. Pure nondual awareness is not an unconscious state, but for people not familiar with rigpa, the experience is nothing but a blackout. For the practitioner with some stability in rigpa, the fourth moment, the ground luminosity which is the same as the primordial purity of dharmakaya, contains the great possibility of enlightenment. To attain stability of awareness in that very moment is complete enlightenment.

If there is no real stability, the four additional very subtle dissolution stages take place: space dissolving into luminosity, luminosity into wisdom, wisdom into union, and union into spontaneous presence. These four belong to the bardo of dharmata.

The first, space dissolving into luminosity, means that the oblivious state becomes awake again. Luminosity means cognizant, not a state of blank void; it is waking up.

The next, luminosity dissolving into wisdom, means that this luminous wakefulness manifests as the fourfold wisdoms. There are only four wisdoms present at this point: the fifth, which is the all-encompassing wisdom, is missing because of not yet having perfected the path. Also, it is said that the all-encompassing wisdom is like the background for the other four. Experientially, what takes place at this point is a vision of a huge field of spheres of four colors.

Next, wisdom dissolves into union. Here "union" refers to the bodily forms of deities. At this time all the peaceful and wrathful deities manifest. After that the union dissolves into spontaneous presence. Spontaneous presence means, in this context, the experience of samsara and nirvana appear in terms of the eight gates of spontaneous presence. At this point, all the possibilities of samsara and nirvana appear simultaneously: the dharmakaya fields, sambhogakaya fields and nirmanakaya fields and the six realms of samsara.

This point offers the final chance to attain enlightenment. The practitioner should therefore recognize that the entire display of spontaneous presence is nothing other than the manifestation of primordial purity. Being stable in the primordial purity is described as "dissolved yet unobscured." Dissolved means that all confusion and discursive thinking have vanished. Unobscured means that the wisdom qualities are not covered in any way whatsoever.

Seen from another angle, when taking rebirth into this life at the moment of conception, the first thing that is formed is the life vein, where the operating of the mind expresses itself as the life-sustaining wind. This primary wind is accompanied by the four subsidiary winds. We can picture this by imagining the physical channel as a bamboo shaft. Inside this bamboo shaft the red and white elements are separated or blown apart by the force of the life-sustaining wind confined within the shaft. As long as that wind operates, the two elements are separated and the living organism is sustained. At the moment of death, the life-sustaining wind loses energy and begins to disintegrate while the life vein, the support, also starts to fall apart. When the life-supporting prana slips away, the two elements merge. The true moment of death is when the red and white element meet together at the heart center and the inner breath ceases. This moment is the dividing point between liberation and further confusion, between practitioners and non-practitioners.

It is generally taught that the person with no knowledge whatsoever about the state of rigpa falls unconscious for three and a half days. When dawn breaks on the fourth day, it is as if the person awakens from a deep sleep. He has no idea of what happened, and wonders, "Where am I? What happened?" This is the moment the mind leaves the body. For the non-practitioner the unconscious state of blackness occurs instead of the unfolding of the luminosity of primordial purity of the bardo of dharmata. Due to this blacking out, normal people experience the luminosity of primordial purity only very briefly. They remain nonconceptual but oblivious, so the experience is more or less skipped. But skilled practitioners do not fall unconscious when the three experiences occur at the time of the ground luminosity of full attainment. In three instants—recognizing, developing strength, and attaining stability—they arrive at the primordial state of liberation.

When the ordinary non-practitioner wakes up again after three days, the mind emerges from one of the nine openings of the body. What happens then is as described in the *Tibetan Book of the Dead*. All the various peaceful and wrathful deities appear during a three-week period. The following four weeks are called the bardo of becoming and seeking new rebirth, so altogether the after-death period lasts seven weeks or forty-nine days. But understand that a day here is not defined like our twenty-four hour days. These are meditation days, the length of which is determined by the individual's capacity to remain undistracted in awareness; the moment of recognizing until forgetting again. These so-called days could be extremely brief for normal people.

The opportunity for enlightenment in the bardo presents itself to the kind of people who are 'in-between' practitioners; not the very best practitioners, but also not normal people. The foremost type of practitioner is freed into dharmakaya at the moment of death during the ground luminosity of full attainment, while normal people are unable to realize the nature of their mind in the bardo. After awakening from the state of oblivion, normal beings go through the four very subtle dissolution stages: space into luminosity, luminosity into wisdom, wisdom into unity and unity into spontaneous presence. At this point there is the possibility for the practitioner of medium quality to be liberated into sambhogakaya. A normal person experiences the qualities of spontaneous presence negatively, perceiving the wisdom manifestations as too sharp, too bright. *The Tibetan Book of the Dead* explains how the wisdom manifestations possess an overwhelming brilliance that is so intense that one cannot bear to look at them. Later, when the realms of samsara and nirvana manifest simultaneously, the lights from the six realms of samsara appear more comforting and attractive, luring non-practitioners back into samsaric existence. The bardo of dharmata finishes and then the bardo of becoming unfolds. Before that takes place, there is one last chance for enlightenment in the bardo of dharmata, when the eight gates of spontaneous presence manifest. The practitioner who recognizes awareness at that point will be able to emanate nirmanakayas, just like the single sun shining in the sky. One sun can manifest simultaneously throughout the world on countless bodies of water. In the same way the buddha activity of manifesting for the benefit of beings is unceasing and all-pervasive, which is the meaning of attaining the sambhogakaya state in the bardo of dharmata.

To prepare for the bardo state, it is very important to keep this thought always in mind: "Whatever I experience right now, whatever happens, is unreal, illusory." Such training will make it much easier to remember the same thing during the bardo states. The most crucial point, however, is to resolve on and rest in the state of rigpa, the nature of mind. Whether the world turns upside down or inside out, it doesn't matter: just lean back and rest in rigpa. We don't have to pigeonhole every single little experience that takes place as being such-and-such, because there is no end to the ideas that dualistic mind can make. It is not at all necessary to categorize all these things. It's more important just to resolve to recognize rigpa no matter what takes place.

What happens during the bardo states is excruciatingly intense, far more so than what we go through right now in our daily life. The sounds are perceived like one million thunderclaps roaring simultaneously. The light is as intense as one hundred thousand suns blazing in the clear sky, and the wrathful apparitions are immeasurable in size, as huge as Mount Sumeru. Actually, the deities are the expression of the nature of our own mind. There is nothing external to try to escape from. The sounds are our own sounds, the colors are our own colors, and the lights are our own lights. Since all these manifestations appear from oneself, they should be recognized as such. The individual who knows this will not be afraid.

Also, it's not really certain in which sequence all these experiences will take place at death. The order they occur in is totally dependent upon the individual person, and there is no way to really generalize. The reason for this is that the innate nature of dharmata is immeasurable, inconceivable. It does not align to any conceptual thinking, so anything can manifest in any order. The experiences can start with the small, increase, then finally vanish, or they can start with the overwhelming presences and dissolve back into the small. There is no way to predict in what sequence the appearances will take place. But if one can just rest in rigpa free from concepts, it doesn't matter in what order the experiences occur.

Whatever is experienced should be dealt with free from expectation, hope or fear. All appearances are nothing other than the mind's manifestations. If there were something real or material to be experienced as 'other', we could reasonably be either afraid or attracted. For the practitioner who knows appearances to be insubstantial, the play of his own mind nature, there is nothing to worry about.

The trouble starts when we perceive immaterial and non-concrete appearances as being real and solid. It is the same as being haunted by a nightmare. The dream is completely unreal but still we attach substantiality to it. To have the same attitude during the death experience will certainly create problems. Like the dream state, everything in the bardo state is immaterial and unreal, like forms of space. How can space harm space?

It's easy to understand this. A real tiger can right now attack and kill us; this is actually possible. That's because it's a physical tiger and we have a physical body. But the bardo experiences are not physical, they are immaterial, insubstantial. To believe they could harm us would be like believing that a drawing of a tiger could eat us—incredibly stupid. In the bardo state things do visibly appear, but without any concreteness or solid reality to them. The body that we have in the bardo state is an illusion of what we habitually believe it to be. There isn't a real, physical body made up of material elements. At that time our body is like a rainbow, and cannot be killed or harmed by anything whatsoever. It's only our belief that we can be hurt that makes the problem. It's not like a real flesh-and-blood tiger coming to eat us.

There is a story about a practitioner in Kham who had practiced a teaching known as illusory body, one of the *Six Doctrines*, for a long time. He had become accustomed to the idea that his body was just illusory, like a magical apparition. One day a boulder dislodged from high up on the mountain and was rolling down to where he stayed. He had the sudden insight that the boulder was illusory and his body was also illusory, so how could anything be harmed? He just sat there. Other people saw this huge boulder land right on top of him and roll away, leaving him completely unhurt. Something like this is possible because everything is created by mind to begin with, and the mind is like a jewel mine: anything can appear from it. There are other stories of meditators confronted by tigers or bears. They'd stick a hand into the mouth of the tiger or bear to see if this thing was just a magical apparition, thinking "Nothing can be harmed!", and for some reason there was no harm. My own root guru told me these stories.

Milarepa proclaimed he was a yogi who had perfected the practice of illusory body and the understanding that everything is like a magical apparition. That's why he could walk straight through the solid rock walls of his cave or exit through the roof and not through the door. One of his chief disciples, Rechungpa, departed from this world through the roof of his cave, leaving a visible opening where originally there was none. He went straight to the celestial realms without leaving a physical body behind. This is only possible by combining the yoga of the illusory body with Mahamudra. The *Six Doctrines* are called the path of means. Mahamudra is the path of liberation. Practicing the path of means without uniting it with the path of liberation does not result in those attainments; it's only when the view of Mahamudra is joined with the path of means that these are possible.

That which takes rebirth is nothing other than what right now feels happy or sad. It is not our body or speech that takes rebirth but our mind, saddled with its past mental imprints and habitual karmic patterns. When we dream, we feel like we have a body moving around, Perhaps we dream we are being chased or eaten by a tiger. None of that is really happening, even though in our confusion we think it is. Exactly the same sort of thing takes place after death. Due to confusion, we think that a lot of things occur while in actuality they don't. Unfortunately we have no real power of choice as to what we perceive at this time. What we experience is in accordance with our karmic imprints. After death, our mind as 'the experiencer' is construed as being in a body. Although it is only a mental body, we habitually imagine we have a physical body. Everything from the moment of death until we enter a new womb is directed by the power of our own past karmic imprints. Of course, if we have some stability in practice certain methods and instructions can be applied, but for the most part there is not any free will. These habitual patterns are the power of karma that forces our immaterial mind to take a material rebirth.

From the point of view of ultimate truth, the acts of dying, taking rebirth, and experiencing this life are nothing more than superficial reality. There is a traditional analogy of two people: one fell asleep and is dreaming, the other did not fall asleep and is not dreaming. Sentient beings are like the person who fell asleep and dreamed a myriad of different experiences, including dying and being reborn. The buddhas are like the person who did not fall asleep and does not have those dreams. The moment one wakes up again, where are all the dreams? They are completely gone, leaving no trace. That is the difference between the enlightened state and the deluded state of a sentient being.

The teachings on ultimate truth never mention that the buddha nature died or was reborn. The nature of mind, which is in fact the state of the primordial buddha Samantabhadra, is beyond birth and death. But sentient beings within the dream state of samsaric existence do experience the illusion of death and rebirth. In that sense there is death and rebirth.

Our essential nature is the same as Samantabhadra's. Truly we are beyond death, we don't die and we aren't reborn; yet it seems like we do. Without truly dying we believe that we die; without truly being reborn it appears to us as if we take rebirth. What actually happens is the same as if we dreamt last night that we died and were reborn: was that real or not?

We have never truly awakened from the sleepy state of primordial ignorance, but when we recognize the natural face of awareness, in a glimpse, it is as if we are just about to wake up. It is like having a light sleep in the morning, one is not completely awake yet. In fact we are still dreaming, because apart from that glimpse of awareness, we take everything as being totally real and concrete, just like a person who believes his dream experience is definitely happening.

All dreams take place within the sleeping state, the framework of sleep. In the same way, all our pleasure and pain, hope and fear, whatever we experience right now during the waking state—the world, ourselves, and other people—all these take place within the framework of dualistic mind. All the drama and display of dualistic mind are the reflection of the buddha nature. As long as we believe that the experiences of dualistic mind are real, we wander endlessly in samsaric existence. This is not the case with the primordial Buddha Samantabhadra. He never fell asleep to begin with, so how could he have any dreams?

ACTIVITIES AND INFORMATION CONNECTED TO THE LINEAGE OF TULKU URGYEN RINPOCHE

WWW.SHEDRUB.ORG

WWW.BLAZINGSPLENDOR.COM

Here you can find contact addresses for teachings and retreats, archives and publications, downloadable pictures to use as screen savers on your computer, biographies of the lineage masters, a more extensive glossary and suggested reading.

9 789627 341598